ULTIMATE
JOB
SEARCH

FOURTH EDITION

LYNN WILLIAMS

First published in Great Britain and the United States as *The Ultimate Job Search Book* in 2006 by Kogan Page Limited.
Second edition published in 2008 as *Ultimate Job Search*
Third edition published in 2012
Fourth edition 2015

2nd Floor, 45 Gee Street
London EC1V 3RS
United Kingdom
www.koganpage.com

1518 Walnut Street, Suite 1100
Philadelphia PA 19102
USA

4737/23 Ansari Road
Daryaganj
New Delhi 110002
India

© Lynn Williams, 2006, 2008, 2012, 2015

ISBN   978 0 7494 7415 7
E-ISBN   978 0 7494 7416 4

British Library Cataloguing-in-Publication Data

A CIP record for this book is available from the British Library.

Typeset by Graphicraft Limited, Hong Kong
Print production managed by Jellyfish
Printed and bound by CPI Group (UK) Ltd, Croydon, CR0 4YY

CONTENTS

20 Offers and rejections   244

INTRODUCTION

Changing jobs rates as one of life's most stressful experiences. However, few of us are still doing the same job we went into after school or college, so it's an event most of us have to cope with at one time or another. How can you make the most of each job move despite economic ups and downs, ensuring you get the job you want, rather than one that will just about do?

Work fills a good one-third of our lives; it's what most of us do all day, every day until retirement. Who wants to spend a third of their day unfulfilled and unhappy in a job they don't like? Yet most of us resist change of any kind, especially dramatic career shifts, even though dissatisfaction at work affects all aspects of our lives, spilling over into our personal lives so our spouses and children feel the effects, too. Being unhappy at the office can also affect our physical health.

This book can help you get the job you want. It can't give you the technical skills or training you need – that's up to you, there are enough colleges and vocational courses out there. What it does give you is the job search skills and techniques that take the stress out of job hunting and make sure your job applications meet with a positive response.

It doesn't matter how weak or strong the economy is, job hunting is a demanding task. This is true even when there is low unemployment and skill shortages. Even during boom times, the average job search takes around three months. Knowing what you're doing during the ins and outs of the recruitment process, remaining optimistic, positive and confident are even more important when times are tough.

You only look for a job a few times in your life. Compared with the amount of time you spend actually doing it you can see that investing time and energy in an effective job search repays the effort many times over. Studies show that people who understand and do well at the job search process enjoy substantially more job satisfaction and higher earnings over the course of their careers. Attention put into the job search can bring not just a more satisfying life but extra salary.

However, because it's something people don't do that often, it's an area in which we often have very little experience. Few people are born knowing how to write a CV, or how to make an impression at an interview. This book is for everyone going through a job change, or even just thinking about it. It will be of use to anyone considering a change to something better, looking for a first job, or forced to change jobs as a result of redundancy or dismissal. It guides you through those fundamental questions about finding a great job:

- How do I start?
- Where do I look?
- What do I do first?

You will find out how to:

- pinpoint exactly what the job requires;
- write a brilliant CV and covering letter;
- handle CV problems without fibs or omissions;
- turn application forms to your benefit;
- identify the best job search strategy for you and get the best out of it;
- use the internet to your advantage;
- understand aptitude and psychometric tests;
- create a great impression at interviews:
  - deal with interview questions, especially the tricky ones;
  - understand what the interviewer is asking and why;
  - prepare and adapt suggested answers well before the interview;
- negotiate job offers;
- handle rejection.

Each chapter ends with quotes from people who are on the receiving end of job applications. This is what employers actually think and feel and what they wish they could tell all would-be applicants. Take their comments on board and you could soon find yourself not just applying for jobs confidently, but actually being offered the job of your dreams.

1
First things first

Applying for a job can seem very daunting, but the actual process can be broken down into several easy stages. To make a good, convincing application, the basic things you have to do are:

1 Find out what skills, qualities and abilities the job requires.

2 Match those skills, qualities and abilities with your own.

3 Prepare examples of how, when and where you have demonstrated them in the past.

4 Present those skills, qualities and abilities clearly and confidently both in writing and verbally.

5 Demonstrate in your presentation, appearance and behaviour the personal qualities required.

Whether you are planning your long-term career, looking for your first job, answering advertised vacancies or applying on spec through your network, the fundamental process is the same. The aim of a job application, from CV to interview, is to convince an employer that you can do the job. If you follow all the steps outlined above, everyone you contact should be able to grasp immediately that you understand exactly what the job requires and that you have the skills, qualities and experience to do it.

Preparing for your job search

To go through these steps requires thought, planning and groundwork. As a bonus, though, the confidence and assurance that you gain from preparing thoroughly will help you enormously, especially when it comes to keeping calm and performing confidently at the interview.

1. Find out what skills, qualities and abilities the job requires

There are several ways of finding out what's needed in a job, and the more familiar you become with these requirements, the better. Knowledge is power, especially when you are applying for jobs. You can get all the information you need from:

- job advertisements;
- job specifications and descriptions;
- your own knowledge and experience;
- the knowledge and experience of others.

Job advertisements

A well-written job advertisement will tell you the skills, qualifications and experience needed for the job. Look at a variety of ads for the sort of job you want, online or in newspapers or journals. By studying a number of them, you will get a clearer idea of the standard requirements, and the range of skills and experience required. You will also notice things that are out of the ordinary, and see where your own unique skills and experience can be of use. Look at as many as possible. As you are not at this stage actually applying for them, practical considerations need not count:

- Do a country-wide internet search, don't just stick to your local area.
- If the site will let you, go back through previous ads.
- Study back issues of newspapers from your local library.
- Do the same with journals and periodicals.

Pick out the significant features. Look for:

- specific skills;
- qualifications and training;
- personal qualities and characteristics;

- knowledge areas;

- areas of experience;

- responsibilities;

- abilities.

Make a list of these key requirements and add any other points. If the ad mentions a company car, for example, assume a full, clean driving licence would be necessary.

Add to the list as you find more ads. Put a mark by characteristics that come up frequently: they are important qualities desired by a wide range of employers. This way, you can get a clear, well-rounded picture of the job you want. See page 19 for more advice on job advertisements.

Job specifications and job descriptions

A job specification is the list of requirements – skills, experience, personal qualities and so on – that define a particular job. It contains much more detail than a job ad, and advertisements are often based on job specifications. Job descriptions are very similar: the terms are often interchangeable, but job descriptions sometimes contain more detail about actual duties and responsibilities.

You can ask companies for copies of job specifications or descriptions, and they can also be accessed from online job search sites and employers' websites.

As with job ads, go through them picking out the significant features to build an even more detailed picture of what the job requires.

Your own knowledge and experience

If you are already doing a similar job, you will have a thorough knowledge of the duties and responsibilities entailed and the skills you need to perform them. Explore your experience, thinking back over what you have done: your everyday duties, the challenges you have faced and what you have achieved. Note down the skills you have developed, and draw up your own job description based on your own know-how.

The knowledge and experience of others

If the job is new to you – it's your first job or you are planning a career change – talk to people who have some knowledge and experience of it. They will be able to give you lots of information, including the personal angle.

People rarely mind being approached, as long as they have time, and will often be flattered to be asked for their opinion, especially if you make it clear that you are asking for information and advice rather than fishing for a job.

By using the methods above, you can build up a clear, well-rounded picture of what employers are looking for, and what the ideal candidate will have. The next step is to assess how well you fit the picture.

2. Match those skills, qualities and abilities with your own

Make a complete list of what's required for the job: the skills, qualifications, qualities and characteristics necessary to fulfil the role to perfection. Now look at your own skills and experience. Consider everything that has helped you develop useful attributes, including:

- your current job;

- jobs you have had in the past;

- unpaid positions such as work experience, voluntary work, community work and sports teams;

- hobbies and interests, including travel;

- your personal life.

List the skills, qualifications and experience you have, and match them to the job requirements. See page 19.

What if there are skills and abilities you don't have?

Check *all* your experience. Although skills acquired in the workplace are valuable, there is nothing to stop you including anything that has helped you develop the skills required.

Can you offer something similar? Different qualifications or training may cover some of the same ground, or you could offer experience in place of academic qualifications. If your experience is in a different but related field, note down the similarities.

Can training or work experience provide the missing skills? Are you willing to do it in your own time, possibly at your own expense, or is training available in your current position? Could you take on extra responsibilities or duties to give you the experience you need?

What if you have skills or experience that aren't relevant?

Can you *make* them relevant? How could they be of use in the job you want to do? Consider thoroughly before discarding them from your CV. They could be 'added extras' that make you an attractive candidate. On the other hand, don't clutter your application with irrelevancies that stop the key points from standing out loud and clear.

3. Prepare examples of how, when and where you have demonstrated them in the past

Study your list of skills and write down details of actual occasions when you have used each one.

It's vital you write it down. It's easy to overlook things if you just think to yourself 'I've done this' or 'I can do that'. What you are looking for, and what you need to present in your CV and at interview, is evidence of your competence – times you have demonstrated the skills required. It's the bedrock on which your application is based.

Make sure you have at least one first-rate example for each requirement. See Chapter 15, 'Interviews: making a great impression'.

4. Present those skills, qualities and abilities clearly and confidently both in writing and verbally

Present your skills in your CV

From analysing job ads and profiles, you know exactly what the employer wants. So you can highlight the important information in your CV, minimize what's not so important, and the employer can see at a glance what a suitable candidate you are. Because you have done your research:

- **You know what to put in, and what to leave out**. Include all your relevant skills and qualities. Focus on these so that the employer can see what you have to offer instead of wading through irrelevancies.

- **You know which areas of experience to focus on**. In your employment history, concentrate on jobs that have provided desirable qualities and experience, giving them the highest prominence.

- **You know what the important details are**. Reflect what's wanted. For example, if the job needs excellent communication skills, include the duties and responsibilities of your previous jobs that reflect those abilities: meeting customers, dealing with enquiries, and so on.

- **You know what training counts**. Concentrate on the training, academic or on the job, that has given you the expertise required.

There's more information about writing a brilliant CV in later chapters.

Present examples at interview

All interviewers are going to be interested in the skills and qualities asked for in the job ad or the job profile, and will base their questions around them. Prepare in advance: know when, where and how you have demonstrated the abilities required, and have ready a good example for each.

For instance, if the job ad says, 'must be able to work under pressure', the interviewer will almost certainly ask how you would cope under pressure. Rather than say you would manage, or you think you would handle it all right, give a real example of a difficult situation you dealt with effectively. For example, an important order that had to be completed to a very tight time limit. Include details of how you stayed calm, got organized and prioritized your workload so that you met the deadline successfully, resulting in further orders. Polish your examples and rehearse them until you can deliver them confidently.

There's more information about interviews and interview techniques later in the book.

5. Demonstrate in your presentation, appearance and behaviour the personal qualities required

Reflect your personal qualities in every contact with prospective employers, whether it's your CV, phone calls or e-mails, interviews or covering letters. The personal qualities that rank highly with employers include:

- **Professionalism**. Make sure everything you do – your CV, application form, covering letter – is of the highest standard: clean, smart and free from careless errors.

- **Enthusiasm**. Display an interest in the jobs you are applying for and the companies offering them.

- **Confidence**. A well-founded belief in yourself and the value of your skills is essential. If you don't think you can do a good job, why should anyone else?

- **Energy**. Be motivated and open to challenge. Return calls promptly; follow up requests for your CV, and be positive and 'can do' about arranging meetings, presentations and interviews. Develop a proactive attitude.

We'll look at all these qualities in a lot more detail in the next chapter where we'll be considering what makes for a highly employable candidate and how you can ensure that you stand out as one.

In the rest of this book we look at job hunting skills in detail: writing CVs, making the most of covering letters, preparing for interviews, handling psychometric tests effectively, and all the other things that ensure you will approach employers with confidence and poise and land the job you want.

2
The highly employable candidate

What makes someone stand out?

What an employer increasingly looks for in a candidate is the guarantee that they will actually deliver what they promise. What they are looking for is evidence of 'employ-ability', and employability is different from your qualifications, skills or experience – it's about your attitude, behaviour and personal qualities. The highly employable candidate can demonstrate they're a dependable team player and will be a fully contributing member of any organization they join.

The question today isn't 'Can you do the job?' but 'Will you do the job?'

What every employer wants

What businesses want from all their employees – from the head of the board to the lowliest shelf-stacker – is:

- **contribution** – the willingness to give that bit extra, to make a difference
- **cultural fit** – an appreciation of the aims and values of the organization, to care about what they care about

- **motivation** – energy, drive and ambition on behalf of oneself, the team and the organization as a whole
- **engagement** – a willingness to take on responsibility, to meet people, problems and opportunities more than half way

These are the things that make businesses successful. They ensure that organizations grow and thrive and that everybody stays employed.

Why are they so important? Because an organization where everyone moves in the same direction will move faster and more easily than one where people pull in different directions or stand still. Shared values matter because when everyone agrees that customer service, for example, is a highly placed value and *every* employee genuinely brings that value into *every aspect* of the business, they are fundamentally more successful than a business that just pays lip service to the concept.

Few businesses have been as successful as Apple Inc. Steve Jobs, its late CEO, said: 'Find people who are competent and really bright, but more importantly, find people who care about exactly the same things you care about.' More and more employers are following his way of thinking, which means they look for personal qualities in their staff that guarantee they'll deliver these requirements. You can train people to do specific tasks – what you can't train them to do is be enthusiastic, proactive, innovative and to really, really care about what they do.

A guarantee of professionalism

So how does an employer ensure that a new employee will fit in, contribute, engage and be motivated? They look for the personal qualities that pretty much guarantee a professional approach. These personal qualities are:

Likeability – warmth, friendliness, agreeableness, cooperation and a degree of emotional intelligence.

People with good good 'likeability skills' – interpersonal and communication skills – are essential. All jobs are essentially customer- or client-focused, whether that means external clients such as the public, or internal clients such as another department, so poor client interactions are a disaster for any company. As well as that, most work these days is done in teams rather than by individuals and teams that don't work well together create big problems.

Employees who are fundamentally agreeable, cooperative, supportive and sociable contribute hugely to the successful operation of their team, the department and, ultimately, the company.

Intelligence – curiosity, common sense and practicality.

People who trust their intelligence are confident about what they undertake – they can analyse situations accurately and make informed choices, as well as having the ability to make decisions and take appropriate action.

We're not talking about super-braininess here, just the ability to use common sense and engage with problems and opportunities – rather than taking a 'don't know, don't care' attitude – and to be willing to learn and to use what you've learned to try new approaches to problems. This means you'll remain motivated and engaged, and able to make a significant contribution.

Competence – responsibility, initiative, reliability and dependability.

Competent employees take responsibility. They can be thoroughly relied on to deliver what is needed when it's needed, capably and to the best of their ability.

The importance of this quality goes without saying, but it's not just having the technical skills to deliver this sort of service that's important, it's having the attitude and will to do so as well.

Integrity – honesty, openness, scrupulousness, congruence.

Successful companies operate in an atmosphere of trust. Teams can't thrive where members don't trust each other, and departments don't work when managers continually check up on their staff. Similarly, the public, clients and customers have to have confidence in the company. After events of the past few years, the slightest hint of dishonesty will cause an immediate haemorrhage of clients. So the company is fundamentally reliant on the integrity of its staff if it is to remain in business.

Positivity – energy, proactivity, confidence, a 'can do' attitude.

Positive people aren't just happier and more cheerful to have around; they perform better too, bringing passion and enthusiasm to the job. They expect positive results, so are willing to go the extra mile and more likely to persist in the face of obstacles. Even better, positive attitudes are catching and positive people inspire and motivate others – which is valuable because positivity engenders creativity and fresh ideas, which is what businesses rely on in order to thrive.

Adaptability – flexibility, the ability to grow and change to meet demands.

Change in the workplace is normal, so companies want employees who look for ways to make it work rather than complain that it won't.

With continuous changes in technology, business practice, markets, economies and society in general, they need people who can shift priorities, adapt to new methods, take on new responsibilities, find ways around obstacles and generally respond positively to fluctuating circumstances.

Adaptable people ensure the success of the organization as it evolves to meet new circumstances – from being flexible enough to handle the daily give-and-take required for working in a team, to responding with energy and poise to major crises.

In a recent survey by a US college, 90 per cent of the employers they contacted rated these sorts of workplace skills as 'important' or 'very important'. Compare this with the 25 per cent who put academic credentials alone in this top bracket. Similarly, a survey conducted by the UK Institute of Directors discovered that 88 per cent of employers considered these personal qualities to be as important or more important than academic ones.

Make full use of every opportunity to demonstrate that you have the required personal qualities. Do your research – find out what the company interviewing you cares about. If the website mentions customer service in every paragraph, that's a very strong clue. What are the skills and personal qualities most needed for first-rate customer service? Make sure they're in your CV. How can you demonstrate in an interview that you are someone customers will like and trust? By being a person the interviewer likes and trusts.

We'll concentrate throughout the rest of this book on making sure all your relevant skills, competencies and experience are presented strongly and clearly. We will also look out for every opportunity to demonstrate these personal qualities, attitudes and behaviours so that you come across as a highly employable candidate – one whom the company will be delighted to have on board and whose colleagues will be glad to work with.

3
Making a start

Your CV, or application form, and the covering letter you send off are your first contact with an employer. If they don't make an impression they may be your last contact as well. You have to get it right first time, every time.

As we saw in previous chapters, when you're applying for a job you need to:

- understand what skills, qualities and abilities the job requires;

- match those skills, qualities and abilities with your own;

- prepare examples of how, when and where you have demonstrated them in the past;

- present those skills, qualities and abilities clearly and confidently both in writing and in person at the interview.

So how does that information help you write a brilliant CV, or fill out an attention-getting application form? A good place to begin is with all the skills and abilities you currently use, and with the skills and abilities you used in other jobs or occupations that could be relevant to what you want to do.

What are the tasks and responsibilities of your job? You know what you do, but how can you tell potential employers so that they have a clear picture too?

Start by listing all the tasks your job involves, then go through them and list the skills, knowledge and abilities you use to accomplish each one. Include specific qualifications and training where appropriate, and add your achievements, too.

Think of it as a particularly thorough warming-up exercise. Only the relevant parts will actually end up in your CV or being discussed at interview, but thinking about what you do and the skills you use to do it will often uncover things you hadn't really thought about before. Most importantly, it will give you a rich tapestry to pick and choose from when you match your skills to the requirements of the job you're applying for. You only need to do it once and the effort is well worth it.

Example

Key task: preparing letters

Skills	Keyboard; Microsoft Word
Abilities	Speed and accuracy
Knowledge	Grammar; mail-merge; database
Qualifications and/or training	IT training
Results and achievements	Prepared 200-letter sponsorship mailout

You can do this for every key task your job involves. If you feel stuck or think you don't have enough, or too much, to put down, think about the following points.

Key tasks

When defining your key tasks, think about everything you have to deal with in your job, including things such as:

- people:
  - clients and customers;
  - colleagues;
  - supervisors;
  - subordinates;
- money and financial procedures;
- products or merchandise;
- technical processes;
- procedures;
- ideas;
- facts and figures;
- communication;
- legal requirements.

Skills, abilities and knowledge

Think about all the things you use to fulfil each of these tasks – the skills and abilities you've developed, along with the knowledge you've gained. What specific skills have you gained through training and what have you acquired through experience?

Consider your:

- learnt skills such as:
  - technical skills;
  - professional skills;
  - communication skills;
  - IT skills;
- natural abilities such as:
  - interpersonal and people skills;
  - creative talent;
  - problem-solving and analytical abilities;
- knowledge and experience, such as:
  - knowledge of processes and procedures;
  - industry knowledge;
  - experience with specific situations and requirements.

Qualifications and training

Consider everything that is relevant to the job you do or intend to do. Don't stop at academic qualifications; include all the vocational training you've had, on-the-job training, short courses, evening classes and workshops, distance and correspondence courses, certification of prior learning.

If it has enhanced your skills, abilities or knowledge, include it. If it means an outside body has passed you as competent to do something, include that, too.

Results and achievements

Think about the results of what you have done in each of these tasks and what you have achieved. Consider the positive effect you've had in your job and include anything that you might have:

- increased, such as:
  - profits;
  - turnover;
  - sales;
  - efficiency;
  - customer satisfaction;
  - market opportunities;
- decreased, such as:
  - staff turnover;
  - risk;
  - complaints or returns;
  - time taken;
  - problems;
  - costs;
  - waste;
- improved, such as:
  - competitive advantage;
  - appearance or marketability;
  - organization;
  - information flow;
  - staff performance;
  - teamwork;
  - relationships, internal or external.

Don't forget any awards or commendations you have won, either individually or as part of a team, and include any promotions you achieved.

Don't feel you necessarily have to stick to workplace-based tasks and responsibilities. If you have little or no work experience – if it's your first job, you're changing career, or you're returning to work after a long break – make full use of other areas of your experience such as voluntary work, studying, travel, household management, team sports, hobbies and interests. Carry out the same key task assessment and you'll find valuable skills and experience you can use.

Transferable skills

As you list your abilities you'll probably notice several that crop up in more than one situation – things like communication skills, computer skills, planning decision-making and problem-solving skills. These are often called 'transferable skills' because they are precisely that: you use them in a variety of tasks.

If you have them, you can adapt them to fit what is required, making them useful across a range of different jobs. They are particularly useful if you are changing careers or looking for your first job when your work experience might be in an unrelated field – see Chapter 7, 'CVs with special considerations', for more information about how you can mine your experience for transferable skills.

You can be as general or as specific as you need to be about your transferable skills, depending on the requirements of the job you're applying for and how well your skills and experience match. For example, you may have just generalized 'computer skills' gained from everyday use; 'computer skills gained in an office environment' if you have done general office work but nothing specific; or you might have 'knowledge of Microsoft Office including Word and PowerPoint' if your skills are specific. Like all skills, be sure you can provide examples of when and where you have used them effectively.

We'll be looking at other aspects of transferable skills in Chapter 4, 'The skills they want from everyone', but before that, what do you do with all this information about your skills and abilities?

Match the skills you've got to the skills they want

Now you have a comprehensive list of all your relevant skills, abilities and knowledge, use them to customize your CV and covering letter so that you stand out as the ideal candidate for the job you're applying for.

Match the skills you've got to the skills the employer wants. Few CVs, application forms or covering letters are read in depth in the first instance. Most are given only a brief scan to see if they might reward further interest. Make it easy to pick you out of the broad mass of applications by emphasizing the most important information – the skills that match the employer's requirements. Don't swamp the key facts with unnecessary details.

How do you get the best match between what your potential employer wants and what you've got to offer? Make full use of all your sources of information:

- the job ad;
- the job description;

- your own knowledge of the job;

- other people's knowledge of the job.

The more information you have the better idea you get of what the job needs. Use your knowledge as the basis for an informed, intelligent application that should impress the employer and put you on the interview list.

Using an advertisement to improve your CV

There is often valuable information in the job advertisement that you can use to make your CV stand out and make it easy to pick you for the interview. It can help you to polish and focus what you include so that you present the best possible match with what the employer is asking for.

Reading the advertisement

PERSONAL ASSISTANT

A small city-based environmental charity requires an experienced, mature assistant to provide administrative and secretarial support. Must have excellent organizational abilities and keyboard skills – Microsoft Office Suite currently used. Good communication skills and a confident telephone manner essential as will be dealing with enquiries from the public. Knowledge of bookkeeping and familiarity with spreadsheets would be an advantage, but training will be given to the right applicant. Understanding of environmental issues desirable. Must be able to work on own initiative without supervision.

They want:

- administrative and secretarial experience;

- computer skills – preferably Microsoft Office;

- maturity – either in age or attitude;

- the ability to organize;

- good communication skills;

- confident telephone manner;

- ability to work on own initiative without supervision.

They would prefer:

- some bookkeeping experience;

- familiarity with spreadsheets;

- experience of dealing with the public;

- understanding of and sympathy with environmental issues.

From your own knowledge and experience of working for a small organization, for example, you can also deduce that they'd like someone who is:

- dependable and supportive;

- willing to learn – they offer extra training if needed;

- flexible and adaptable;

- helpful;

- able to do routine office work efficiently but able to cope with responsibility when the need arises.

A good match to these requirements – don't forget to dig through *all* your skills, abilities and experience – should put you on the interview list.

Putting it in your CV

See Chapter 5 for more detailed information about writing your CV, but before you do consider how you might use your knowledge of the employer's requirements to strengthen *any* CV you put together. Once you know what they want, you can make good use of that information by:

- using key words and phrases that appear in the advertisement;

- selecting from your range of skills the ones specifically mentioned;

- giving preference to good skill matches;

- including all your relevant qualifications and experience.

Example CV

Name

Address

Contact details

Personal profile

Write a profile using the key words that appear in the advertisement.

Experienced, confident office administrator and secretary with excellent organizational skills gained in supporting several small and medium-sized organizations and a background in dealing with customer enquiries

Key skills

Include all your skills and qualifications that are mentioned in the advertisement:

- Six years' experience in administrative and secretarial positions
- Computer skills
  - Word
  - Outlook Express
  - Excel spreadsheet package
- Bookkeeping experience
- Excellent communication skills
- Confident telephone manner
- Able to work on own initiative
- Able to prioritize and organize workload

Career history

  - Dates, Employer
  - Administrative Assistant

Link your duties and responsibilities to the ones requested along with those you believe would be useful in the situation described. Use them to support your key skills and include, for example:

Provided administrative and secretarial support to department

- Dealt with general office administration
- Word processed letters and reports
- Dealt with incoming mail
- Dealt with calls and enquiries to the department
- Maintained department diary – organized and coordinated appointments
- Liaised with personnel in other offices

cont

If you have important, relevant experience, don't exclude it just because it's outside the workplace. Include, for example:

- – Dates, Employer
- – Treasurer of Local History Society (voluntary position)
- – Treasurer for 500-strong local organization
- Undertook bookkeeping using Excel spreadsheets
- Maintained accounts
- Prepared books for auditing
  - – Dates, Employer
  - – Retail Assistant

Briefly outline duties and responsibilities, starting with the most relevant:

- Dealing with customers confidently
- Answering enquiries
- Offering help and advice

Education and training

Give details, including, for example:

Dates, College

NVQ level 2 Office Administration

Personal details

Remember to include anything relevant, for instance:

Interests: Member of the Woodland Conservation Volunteer Trust

Think very carefully about what else you add. You need supporting details of your other jobs, duties, qualifications, etc to give a complete picture, but make sure the all-important skills and qualities still stand out clearly. Don't bury them under a lot of irrelevant information.

We'll look at how you can adapt this technique to help you write covering letters and answer interview questions later in this book.

EXPERT QUOTE

If it's in the job description, it *must* be on the form (or CV).

MAGGIE FELLOWS – PROJECT MANAGER, SOUTH WEST TUC

EXPERT QUOTE

When we have a big response for a vacancy, CVs are often sifted by an administrative clerk first. If they don't see the four or five competencies we specifically ask for on the CV, it doesn't get any further.

DEBBIE MACEKE – RESOURCE CENTRE MANAGER, ROLLS-ROYCE

4
The skills they want from everyone

In the previous chapters, as well as looking at specific skills we've also looked at those less easy to define skills such as employability and transferable skills.

While specific skills are easy to recognize and include in your CV, these more nebulous skills can be rather harder to pin down and exhibit. But they are fundamental skills that are useful in almost every job and required by most employers. They may not be mentioned directly in job ads or job descriptions, but are highly desirable none the less.

In reviewing the skills set out below and considering your experience of each of them, you will also be covering a range of valuable employability skills and transferable abilities. They are well-used skills that you could take for granted unless you are asked for them specifically, which is why it's worth reviewing them here and making sure you include them when you write your CV and covering letter, and plan your answers to interview questions.

The skills are:

Teamwork

Have you ever, for example:

- contributed to a team effort?
- helped others within the team achieve their targets?
- resolved conflict or arguments within a team?

Communicating with others

Communication skills include the ability to:

- influence, motivate and persuade people;
- negotiate with others;
- receive and present information and ideas clearly and accurately.

Have you ever, for example:

- handled complaints or dealt with other demanding circumstances?
- listened to the concerns of others – colleagues, supervisors, customers or others – and responded to that information effectively?
- presented information clearly and accurately to groups and/or individuals, in person or in writing?
- put your point of view across to others successfully?

Problem solving

Have you ever, for example:

- noticed a problem and planned how to resolve it?
- foreseen a potential problem and taken steps to avoid it?
- understood how to resolve a problem and persuaded others to take the necessary steps?

Analysing

Have you ever, for example:

- gathered information about something, weighed up the pros and cons and made a decision based on your research?
- weighed up the facts about a situation and made an appropriate judgement?

Organizing and planning

Have you ever, for example:

- prioritized tasks to achieve a target or meet a deadline?
- planned a project through to completion?
- organized an event?
- planned a project or event and delegated tasks to others?

Flexibility and adaptability

This includes the ability to:

- adapt to the demands of the job;
- change and develop;
- multitask.

Have you ever, for example:

- adapted successfully to a changing situation?
- become proficient at a task or skill quickly and effectively?
- become more knowledgeable about your work?
- handled several tasks competently and efficiently?
- reacted appropriately to unexpected situations as they arose?

Drive and determination

Have you ever, for example:

- recovered from a setback or disappointment?
- overcome obstacles?
- achieved results over and above set targets?

Everyone will have experience of using the majority of these skills, if not at work then in other areas of their lives. As we've seen before, employers value them because they ensure that you will be able to carry out the more specific tasks your job entails. You can train people to do a specific task, but you can't train them to do it with drive and determination, for example. And it would be difficult to get any job done without, let's say, communication skills – the ability to follow instructions, liaise with others, negotiate conditions, give feedback and report results.

As before, it's worth actually writing down answers to the questions above as part of your extremely thorough preparation because you only need to do it once and it will remind you of things you hadn't necessarily thought about before as well as giving you ample material to work with when it comes to writing your CV or application form and preparing for interviews. And writing your CV is what we're going to tackle next.

5
Your CV

Your CV needs to:

- attract attention out of dozens or even hundreds of other CVs;

- create a good impression and be professional and businesslike;

- present your relevant skills and qualities clearly and concisely.

The letters CV stand for the Latin *curriculum vitae*, meaning course of life, and early CVs were just that: an outline of someone's career history, listing the places he or she had worked with dates and job titles. These days CVs put the emphasis on skill, experience and achievement, and tell employers what you will be able to do for them rather than just who you have worked for in the past.

Attract attention

The purpose of a CV isn't to get you a job; it's to get you an interview for the job. Don't try to put every detail of your background into your CV: put in what will interest an employer and make him or her want to know more about you. The things employers most want to know are whether you have:

- the specific skills needed for the job;

- the right sort of experience;

- an understanding of what the job requires;

- the personal qualities needed.

With many advertised vacancies attracting hundreds of replies, an employer will spend only seconds scanning each CV. If yours presents these key points at a glance, it stands a greater chance of being read more thoroughly.

Create a good impression

Creating a good first impression isn't difficult. Make your CV look businesslike and professional:

- Keep it short: no more than two pages in short, succinct sections that illustrate your skills and experience.

- Use plain white or cream A4-sized paper: 100 gsm paper has a good weighty high-quality feel to it.

- Print in black and use regular fonts that are easy to read by both human eyes and computer scanners.

- Use wide margins and white space to give a clean, uncluttered look.

- Arrange the information in clearly headlined, easy to read sections.

- Put the most important information on the first page. If you have a two-page CV, make sure the front page is the more interesting and highlights your key skills and achievements.

- Check spelling, grammar and punctuation rigorously. Spellcheckers are not infallible and will not realize that 'there' should be 'their' or 'they're', or that 'fist' should really be 'first'.

- Send your freshly printed CV unstapled and unfolded in a white A4 envelope.

- Include a covering letter written specifically to highlight your suitability for the job – see Chapter 10, 'Covering letters'.

- Send the application in before the closing date, to a named individual, not just 'the Personnel Department'.

Present your relevant skills

CVs contain a lot of information, which can make them confusing to read. The easiest way to keep them uncomplicated is to present everything in short, clearly headed sections that lead the reader logically through the key points. Most CVs contain the following sections:

- contact details;
- personal profile;
- key skills;
- career history;
- education and training;
- personal details.

Contact details

These usually come first on the CV. A potential employer needs to know who you are and how to get in touch with you. Include:

- your name;
- your address;
- your home phone number and/or your mobile number;
- your e-mail address.

Example

John Smith
Flat 1, Any Street
Any Town AA1 1AA
Tel. 00000 000000 Mob. 00000 000000
E-mail:jsmith@anyisp.co.uk

Personal profile

Ideally, the personal profile condenses into a couple of sentences the essence of what you do and how you do it. A short, well-written, well thought-out personal profile gives readers a useful introduction to your abilities, while a lazy profile full of empty clichés and buzzwords will put them off. To plan an effective profile, consider:

- who you are and what you do;

- your significant skills and strengths;

- where you gained them – your essential experience;

- your key personal qualities.

Jot down some key words that sum up each issue. Consider what makes you good at what you do and where your strengths lie. What is likely to be of most interest to a potential employer?

What we've aiming for is a short punchy summary of the professional you.

Example

Who I am and what I do: personal assistant; graduate
Significant skills and strengths: bilingual French/English; office skills; IT skills
Essential experience: working in both France and the UK
Key personal qualities: efficient; personable; good at prioritizing

Finished personal profile:

Personal Profile

A skilled and experienced bilingual PA fluent in business French, having worked for Alliance UK in Paris, and the French company CBC International in England. A highly efficient, personable graduate with excellent office and IT skills, and the ability to prioritize a demanding workload.

Example

Who I am and what I do: computer software trainer
Significant skills and strengths: fully qualified/Microsoft approved
Essential experience: background in data analysis and information management; knowledge of business and financial environments and what they are likely to require from training
Key personal qualities: mature, competent

Finished personal profile:

Personal Profile

Microsoft-approved trainer for PC spreadsheets, data management and graphics presentation software. A mature, competent professional with prior experience in information management and data analysis acquired in a range of business and financial environments.

Example

> *Who I am and what I do:* retail sales – fashion and women's wear
> *Significant skills and strengths:* customer care; colour and design
> *Essential experience:* wide ranging from department store to small/exclusive boutiques
> *Key personal qualities:* creative, versatile, adaptable, intelligent, smart appearance
>
> **Finished personal profile:**
>
> **Personal Profile**
> A smart, intelligent, experienced retail professional with an extensive background in fashion and women's wear in both large department stores and exclusive boutiques. Creative, adaptable and versatile with first-rate customer-care skills, and an excellent sense of colour and design.

Alternatively, you could consider using a summary instead of a Personal Profile. This is an even tighter and more focused way of presenting the information, using bullet points to summarize exactly what you have to offer.

Example

> **Personal Summary**
> ● 5+ years' background in...
> ● Expert knowledge of...
> ● Management of...
> ● Strong experience in...
> ● Experience of...

This approach is especially useful when the breadth and depth of your experience are your strongest attributes – in management roles, for example. It works best when you have something substantial to offer which matches the job requirement exactly.

Key skills

The section that highlights your key skills is the most important part of your CV. Anyone reading it can see at a glance what you have to offer. Use it to emphasize the most important points in your favour, keeping the actual job requirements firmly in mind.

Example

> **Key skills**
> - Supervising staff
> - Implementing standard procedures accurately and efficiently
> - Prioritizing workload
> - Analysing and rectifying errors
> - Computer skills:
>   - Microsoft Word
>   - Excel spreadsheets
>   - Outlook and Explorer e-mail and internet facilities.

Example

> **Key skills**
> - Managing staff in a high-turnover production environment
> - Providing a first-rate engineering service to internal and external customers
> - Five years' experience in project management
> - Budget preparation
> - Training and motivating staff.

This section can also be used to highlight your key qualifications, key experience or significant achievements if these are more appropriate and relevant (see Chapter 8, 'CVs for specific jobs'), whatever is more important.

Example

> **Key qualifications**
> - MSc Psychology of Learning
> - BSc Psychology
>   - Advanced statistical analysis
>   - Quantitative techniques in applied research
>   - Experimental psychology
>   - The psychology of education and development.

Example

> **Key experience**
> - Ten years' experience in project management working in a wide range of environments
> - Sound knowledge of health and safety, and employment legislation and practice
> - Thorough understanding of staff motivation and training
> - A clear commitment to excellence
> - An established track record in effective solutions.

Example

> **Key achievements**
> - Achieving 50 per cent increase in uptake of technical support services
> - Increasing sales by up to 15 per cent annually
> - Heading highly successful, award-winning sales team
> - Attaining:
>   - Diploma in Marketing
>   - Certified Diploma in Accounting and Finance
>   - Diploma in Management Studies.

Career history

This section gives the employer information about your current job, as well as what you have done in the past. For this information to be useful, don't just give company names, job titles and dates. Give details of your main responsibilities and duties, and your key achievements in the role. Start with a sentence that summarizes your responsibilities then itemize the key points with bullet points (see examples). Highlight the advantages of employing you, and include any of the following achievements:

- **Increasing**:
  - productivity;
  - sales or profit;
  - product turnover;
  - efficiency;
  - market opportunity.

- **Improving**:
  - customer relations;
  - design;
  - employee relations;
  - public profile;
  - marketability;
  - information flow;
  - staff performance;
  - team effectiveness.

- **Reducing**:
  - staff turnover;
  - time taken;
  - costs;
  - waste;
  - risk.

Start with your current position and work backwards. Include detailed information about recent jobs – the first two or three in the section – and summarize the rest.

Example

Career history
2011 to present: ABC Ltd

System Controller
Supported 200 staff on six sites throughout the south of England using computerized systems.

- Provided help desk for software and hardware queries.
- Used operating systems to recover lost data files.
- Analysed system performance, identified problems and established probable origin before taking appropriate action.
- Logged errors for both software and hardware, and referred on to either programmer or engineer as appropriate.
- Improved average lost system time from average of 24 hours down to 4 hours.
- Promoted from Claims Supervisor to System Controller after completing City & Guilds Diploma in Computer Application.

cont

2007 to 2011: XYZ Financial Services Ltd

Claims Supervisor

Clerical Officer

Assessed claims for household insurance, supervising up to seven staff members. Maintained cheque issue deadlines and administered insurance certificate stocks.

Example

Career history

2011–present: DEF Primary Health Care Trust

Chef

Worked as member of team providing full meals service within central kitchen preparation unit for large hospital trust producing 5,000 meals a day.

- Prepared meals for consumption within the Trust hospitals and day-care centres.
- Supervised routine food preparation.
- Prepared food with regard to special dietary needs such as diabetic, low salt, low fat, gluten free.
- Undertook preparation of food for chilling and distribution.
- Maintained high quality of preparation and presentation.
- Consistently met annual budgetary targets.
- Cut waste by estimated 15 per cent.

2009–2011: GHI Resources South East

Chef

Assistant Chef

Provided high-quality catering service to staff and visitors for a number of large commercial clients, working both on own initiative and as part of a team.

- Prepared breakfast and lunch for up to 250 people a day.
- Undertook pastry and some confectionery work.
- Delivered hospitality service requiring exceptionally high standards of preparation and presentation.

2007–2009: JKL School

Canteen Cook

Part of four-person team preparing lunchtime meals service for 1,700 children and staff including menu choices and food prepared to special dietary requirements.

Example

> **Career history**
>
> 2013–present: ABC Freetime Project
>
> **Drama Coach**
>
> Worked as part of team to plan and implement out-of-school drama project for 70 mixed-ability students aged 8 to 11.
>
> - Taught performance techniques.
> - Coached and motivated to production standard.
> - Set goals to encourage performance levels.
> - Monitored students' progress.
> - Maintained records.
> - Achieved four productions with near-100 per cent participation – all well received and appreciated by community audience.

Education and training

This is an important section for anyone who has just left school or university. It will include detailed information on courses taken and exams passed. See Chapter 7, 'CVs with special considerations', for more information about CVs for school and college leavers.

Anyone who has been in work for a couple of years, though, will find that workplace credentials become more significant to employers than exam results, so include all relevant workplace training as well as your broader academic qualifications:

- educational achievements: GCSEs, A levels, AS levels, diplomas and degrees;

- professional qualifications;

- technical qualifications;

- relevant vocational training;

- relevant company training programmes;

- IT skills and training;

- language skills;

- relevant professional association membership.

Start with the highest or most relevant qualification and work back. The longer ago it was, the less detail you need to include. If it's a recent and relevant qualification, though, include brief details of what was covered in the course and the skills you attained.

Example

Education and training

2013–present: ABC College

NVQ level 3

Clerical Skills course focusing on administration and supervision. This advanced course updates and enhances my current office management and IT skills.

2003–2005: DEF College of Further Education

College Secretarial Diploma

1996–2003: GHI School

A levels: English, French, Economics

GCSEs: seven including Maths and English

Example

Education and training

Fellow of the Chartered Institute of Personnel and Development

Diploma in Personnel Management

XYZ Business School – 2010

Diploma in Education

RST College – 2003

Work-related training:

- Psychometric testing
- Aptitude testing
- Assessment skills
- Careers guidance and coaching.

Example

> **Education and training**
> ABC College – 2009 to 2011
> **Diploma in Journalism**
>
> XYZ University – 2003 to 2006
> **BA History and English**
> FGH School – 2001 to 2003
> **A levels: English, History, French**
> **GCSEs: Nine, including English and Maths**

Personal details

This section covers your interests and activities, plus any other personal details that are relevant but not important enough to appear in other sections. These include:

- possession of a full clean driving licence;

- date of birth, if you include it;

- nationality and employment status, if relevant;

- a registered disability, if relevant.

Keep details of hobbies and interests brief, and be selective about what you include. Community activities and team games are usually seen as an asset, while membership of political parties, religious groups or controversial special-interest groups (pro- or anti-hunting bodies, for example) should be excluded.

Example

> **Personal details**
> Date of birth: 12 July 1994
> Health: Non-smoker
> Licence: Full clean UK driving licence. Advanced motorist's certificate.
> Interests: Riding and pony-trekking. Assistant at local stable, helping with handicapped children's weekends and holidays.

Example

Personal details

Date of birth: 3 May 1984

Interests: team sports

- netball
- women's league football
- volleyball.

Full clean UK driver's licence

References available on request.

Example

Personal details

Interests: Swimming and sailing

              Member of East Sussex Choral Society

              Member of local parish council

Car owner/driver with clean licence

Non-smoker.

Keep your CV relevant

Make every line count. The more irrelevant stuff you put in your CV, the more difficult it is to pick out the really important facts, so be choosy about what you include. If you think it will help you get an interview, put it in. If you are not sure, consider carefully. Could you use the space for something more important?

You can leave out:

- Unnecessary personal details such as:

  - marital status;

  - maiden name;

  - number and ages of children;

  - nationality;

  - gender;

  - partner's name or occupation;

  - religious affiliation;

  - political affiliation;

  - age and/or date of birth;

  - previous salary;

  - reason for leaving last job.

- Photographs, unless specifically requested.

- Names and addresses for references. If they are needed, they will be asked for.

- Negative information. Never, ever bend the truth on your CV, but think twice about including anything that diminishes your chance of an interview. If it does not affect your ability to do the job, wait until you can explain fully, face to face.

- Out-of-date information. What you are currently doing is more relevant than what you did a decade ago. Edit details of long-ago jobs and qualifications, and use the space for more significant things.

Example CV

Jane Smith
23 Any Street
Anytown AA1 1AA
Tel. 00000 000000
E-mail: jsmith@anyisp.co.uk

Personal profile
An office manager and administrative supervisor with experience in both the private and public sectors, who enjoys the challenge of a busy, demanding work environment, and has the ability to maintain a consistently high standard of work under pressure.

Key skills
- Supervising staff
- Implementing standard procedures accurately
- Prioritizing workload
- Proficient French
- Computer skills – Microsoft Office:
  - Word
  - Excel
  - Outlook
  - PowerPoint.

cont

Career history

2008 to present: ABC County Council

Office Manager

Senior Administrator

Clerical Administrator

Responsible for collation and administration of documents and records.

- Supervised full-time staff of five, plus short-contract and agency staff depending on workload.
- Trained staff in procedures and monitored implementation.
- Motivated and encouraged staff while working to strict deadlines, often under pressure.
- Organized data within the department.
- Dealt with queries to the department.
- Liaised with senior levels.
- Maintained department productivity and high rate of accuracy in all situations.
- Promoted twice within same organization.

2003 to 2008: XYZ Assurance plc

Clerical Administrator

Organized and carried out office administration.

- Dealt with phone enquiries and requests.
- Maintained all department records and files.
- Dealt with incoming mail.
- Prepared routine correspondence.

2001 to 2003: ABC Imports Ltd

Clerical Assistant

Dealt with office administration including bookkeeping and invoicing.

Education and training

2013–present: ABC College

NVQ level 3

Clerical Skills course focusing on administration and supervision. This advanced course updates and enhances my current office management and IT skills.

1999–2001: DEF College of Further Education

College Secretarial Diploma

1991–1999 GHI School

A levels: English, French, Economics

GCSEs: seven including Maths and English

cont

Personal details

Interests: Swimming and sailing

Studying for Coastal Navigation Certificate

Member of Anytown Drama Society

Car owner/driver with full, clean, UK licence

St John's Ambulance First Aid certificate holder

Non-smoker

EXPERT QUOTE

You've got two seconds to get someone's attention – you don't do that with your name and address, you need a personal profile. Summarize your experience and main skills, but don't waste space on bland personal characteristics – everyone is hard-working and ambitious.

I know when I added an experience-based personal profile to my CV I started getting a response immediately.

MARK COLTON, BUSINESS DEVELOPMENT TEAM, JOBCENTREPLUS

EXPERT QUOTE

The reader of your application form or CV can't extrapolate – if information isn't down in black and white it isn't there. Spell it out.

MAGGIE FELLOWS, PROJECT MANAGER, SOUTH WEST TUC

EXPERT QUOTE

Employers often look at hobbies and interests to see what sort of person someone is – a team player, self-motivated, that sort of thing.

MARK COLTON, BUSINESS DEVELOPMENT TEAM, JOBCENTREPLUS

6
CV problems

What if your career history isn't perfect? It can be tempting to bend the truth in your CV to make yourself look better. Resist the temptation. Not only is it dangerous, it's unnecessary. You can often overcome problems by emphasizing some parts of your CV while playing down others.

The purpose of a CV is to get an interview. You do that by demonstrating what's right about you, not what's wrong. You may have to answer searching questions about your background or qualifications when you get to the interview – see Chapter 16, 'Answering interview questions' – but at least you can do it face to face and give a full explanation.

Problem: there are gaps in my career history

Smooth over small gaps by rounding up dates, giving the year rather than month and year – '2008 to 2009' rather than 'November 2008 to January 2009'. For longer gaps, say what you were doing and focus on the skills and achievements you gained. Whether it was training, studying, travelling, doing voluntary work, child-rearing, free-lancing or trying self-employment, there will be something positive and relevant you can use if you look hard enough.

Example

Career history

2008–2009 Travelling in Europe

- Travelled to Spain, France and Portugal
- Developed language skills
- Learned about and gained appreciation of different cultures
- Improved interpersonal skills
- Enhanced problem-solving skills
- Acquired independence.

Problem: my career history isn't straightforward

Make it as straightforward as possible on your CV so that any employer reading it can see clearly what you have to offer. Present the employer with reasons why your career history makes you right for the job. Be selective and organize the information rigorously.

- Summarize the main theme of your experience in your personal profile, bearing in mind the job you are applying for.

- Be selective about what you put in the key skills section. If you have a range of relevant skills, group them under separate headings.

- If your career history is varied, pick out the most relevant experience and summarize the rest.

The writer of the CV on the next page is applying for a job in sales and therefore emphasizes sales skills. If the job was in business management, the CV would stress management skills such as team building, problem solving and budget management.

Problem: my relevant experience is in a voluntary role

The skills and experience you gain from voluntary work are just as real and useful as those gained in the workplace, so put them in. See the example CV in Chapter 3, 'Making a start', for how to include this experience in your career history.

Problem: I've had lots of very different jobs

Your career history may lack direction. Fortunately, most skills are transferable apart from specific technical skills. Most jobs need interpersonal skills or problem-solving skills, for example. Pick relevant transferable skills to put in the key skills section, and add any relevant specific or technical abilities. Summarize your career history, focusing specifically on using these skills.

Useful transferable skills include, along with many others:

- communication and interpersonal skills;

- negotiating and persuasion skills;

- analytical skills;

Example CV

Personal profile

A sales professional with 15 years' experience in both sales and retail, who has significantly increased sales and improved profits in highly competitive markets through the use of highly developed interpersonal skills and a flexible, versatile approach.

Key skills

Sales

- Maintaining and servicing existing accounts while developing new territory, taking it from 5 per cent to 65 per cent of overall turnover in 3 years
- Liaising with distribution department to ensure efficient service to customers, reducing waiting time by two weeks
- Developing new sales drive offering extended range of products to existing customers
- Using sales analysis to target key customers, increasing sales to them by 23 per cent.

Business management

- Recognizing business development opportunities
- Maintaining customer service and satisfaction
- Researching and establishing new market developments
- Identifying and understanding customer needs.

Career history

2011–present: XYZ Gifts

cont

Retail Manager

- Managed busy town-centre gift and special-occasion shop
- Selected and purchased stock
- Developed marketing and promotion
- Developed existing potential and increased profits by 20 per cent above target.

2008–2011: ABC Windows

Sales Representative

- Developed new territory in highly competitive market
- Successfully negotiated and secured sales
- Developed successful sales initiatives to make the most of existing customers.

2005–2008: JKL Ltd

Purchasing Manager

2002–2005: TUV Ltd

Telesales Representative

1999–2002: VWX Ltd

Clerical Assistant

- time-management skills;

- problem-solving and decision-making skills;

- multitasking skills;

- budgeting;

- motivational skills;

- creative skills.

See Chapter 4 for more about the useful skills that most employers want.

Problem: my CV is more than two pages long

A CV more than two pages long looks daunting. Concentrate on your relevant skills, qualifications and experience. Remember your current and recent jobs are the most interesting, and summarize everything else, giving just the main facts and edited highlights. Put the important information on the first page.

Problem: I'm doing more than one job

This situation isn't unusual nowadays, with people doing two or more part-time jobs, or combining self-employment with other work. If one of the jobs is a 'stopgap', ignore it and concentrate on the relevant one. If, however, both jobs are equally important and relevant, include both skill sets in your key skills section, and put both jobs in your career history.

Example

Career history

2011–present: ABC Productions Ltd

Video Trainer and Facilitator

Working with a community youth group

- Assisted group making their own and community videos
- Trained them in use of equipment and basic production and editing techniques
- Coordinated content and storyline and helped them realize their ideas.

ABC Radio

Radio Researcher and Presenter

- Researched, planned and presented weekly community news slot for local radio
- Scripted reports for other presenters
- Selected, approached and interviewed guests.

Problem: I've only ever had one job

Your experience could look thin. Include the full range of skills you have developed and used in that job, along with your knowledge and achievements. Put them in your key skills section or under the duties and responsibilities in your career history. Don't neglect skills and experience you have gained from outside interests or voluntary work.

Example

Personal profile

A well-organized, reliable personal assistant with extensive knowledge of good office practice gained through eight years' experience. Hardworking and reliable, with the ability to remain calm and good-humoured under pressure.

Key skills

- City & Guilds CLAIT
- RSA III typewriting – current speed 70 wpm
- RSA II Audio-typing – current speed 70 wpm
- RSA II Shorthand – current speed 120 wpm
- RSA II Secretarial Studies.

Career history

2006–present: XYZ & Co Ltd

Secretary and PA to Finance Manager

Undertook a full range of secretarial and administrative duties and responsibilities.

Secretarial

Personal Assistant and Secretary to the Financial Manager.

- Full knowledge of Microsoft Office
- Excellent keyboard skills
- Dealing with enquiries face to face and over the phone
- Experienced at:
  - producing reports and correspondence
  - taking and transcribing dictation
  - taking minutes at meetings
  - compiling spreadsheets and reports using MS Excel.

Administrative

Answerable for all secretarial and clerical staff administration for Financial Department

- Responsible for the day-to-day running of department
- Overseeing staff of four
- Coordinating department work schedules
- Organizing client presentations and corporate entertainment
- Training and supervising junior staff.

Problem: a lot of my jobs have been the same

If your duties and responsibilities have been the same in each job, focus on your skills and achievements and summarize your actual career history.

Example

Key skills

- Customer care
- Cash handling and security
- Stock control, including operating computerized stock control system
- Financial administration, including credit agreements, customer accounts, credit/debit notes, and bank reconciliations
- Clerical administration, including sales reports and customer correspondence.

Key achievements

- Organized and managed trade stand at Ultimate Home exhibition for three years
- Used computerized stock control system to track and analyse stock movement between five branches
- Organized daily bank deposits of cash and credit card takings
- Member of an award-winning team – MicroSpec 2006.

Career history

2012–present: ABC Ltd
Sales Demonstrator

2009–2012: XYZ & Co
Sales Consultant

2007–2009: EFG & Son Ltd
Sales Consultant

2005–2007 HIJ Ltd
Sales Assistant

Problem: I've been unemployed for over a year

If you have been in training during that time, or doing voluntary work, trying to start your own business, or bringing up a family, you'll have gained useful skills. If you haven't been doing anything in particular, enrol on a training course or community programme that will help fill the awkward gap.

Add the skills to your key skills section and include what you have been doing in your career history.

Example

Key skills

- Managing staff in a high-turnover production environment
- Providing a first-rate engineering service to internal and external customers
- Project management and budget preparation
- Training and motivating staff.

Career history

2013 to present: ABC Training

Training Supervisor

(Voluntary position)

Trained community project volunteers in basic engineering skills for a variety of projects including environmental and conservation work.

2007 to 2013: DEF Engineering Ltd

Industrial Engineer

Responsible for all industrial engineering services at factory and divisional level. Monitored, coordinated and delivered production engineering service with particular emphasis on product costing, value engineering, pre-production engineering and methods improvement. Provided work measurement facilities and maintained bonus scheme.

Problem: my current job isn't very impressive or relevant, or it's a bit of a step backwards

Focus on your relevant skills rather than your current job. Make full use of your key skills section and add a key experience section as well, or combine the two.

Example

Key skills and experience

- Considerable experience in all aspects of human resource management, assessment and development:
  - Highly skilled in personnel management
  - Developed personnel policies and procedures for financial group
  - Improved effectiveness of human resource development strategies
  - Managed introduction of performance evaluation system
- Extensive contact with training agencies, Training and Enterprise Councils, and employers

cont

- Qualified and experienced in the use of tests:
  - Psychometric testing
  - Aptitude testing
  - Assessment skills
  - Careers guidance and counselling
- Experienced in devising, delivering and assessing training courses
- Thorough knowledge of employment law.

Career history

2011 to present: ABC Ltd
Personnel Officer

2006 to 2011: XYZ Ltd
Human Resources Manager

2002 to 2006: OPQ Ltd
Personnel Officer

1993 to 2002: EFG Ltd
Personnel Assistant
Clerical Officer
Clerical Assistant

Problem: I haven't got much experience for the job I want

Make the most of what you have got. Look at all your experience: qualifications, training, current work experience, voluntary work, transferable skills and personal qualities. If lack of experience is a big obstacle, go back into training or look at other ways of getting it, such as volunteering, work placement, or temporary or part-time work, even if it means taking a step down the career ladder. It may seem daunting but it could be worthwhile in the long run.

Problem: I'm over-qualified

Concentrate on the hands-on skills and practical experience that you use in the job. Put them in your key skills section and focus on them in duties and responsibilities in your career history.

Put your 'excess' qualifications in the education and training section on the second page of your CV.

Problem: I'm under-qualified

You must believe you have the experience to do the job or you wouldn't be applying. Put your key, relevant skills and experience on the front page and include any relevant workplace training even if it's not diploma or degree level.

Problem: I'm over 50

Emphasize your achievements and significant skills. Mention any training you have done to keep them up to date. Give details about your last few jobs and summarize early ones ruthlessly.

Example

Career history

2009 to present: ABC Ltd

Art Director

- Devised concepts and supervised staff in preparing designs for artwork and copy for direct marketing agency
- Consulted with client companies with regard to aims and objectives, presentation and budget
- Formulated layout and design concept
- Produced, selected or arranged to have produced suitable material for artwork and/or illustrations
- Supervised staff preparing layouts for printing
- Approved final layout for presentation to client.

1998–2009: XYZ Ltd

Studio Manager

Assistant Studio Manager

- Assisted organization and running of studio together with production of high-concept computer graphics for audio-visual company
- Created a range of graphics for video and audio-visual presentation
- Supervised allocation of projects
- Briefed and monitored freelance staff.

1993–1998: EFG Ltd

Designer

Produced graphics material for company bulletins, brochures, annual reports and in-house magazines

Prior to 1993: Various

Designer and Paste-up Artist

Produced a variety of graphic material for magazines and brochures.

Problem: I'm under 25

You could be seen as lacking experience. Make the most of what you have got, and highlight all your relevant skills and experience. The answer to the problem 'I've only ever had one job' could be useful.

If this is your first job after further or higher education, see Chapter 7, 'CVs with special considerations', for some ideas on how to compile your CV.

EXPERT QUOTE

Avoid gaps in your CV. If you've been travelling or at home caring for relatives, put it in; don't just miss a bit out of your work history, the employer needs to know there's a reason for it. You'll have developed useful skills whatever you were doing, so put those in.

MARK COLTON, BUSINESS DEVELOPMENT TEAM, JOBCENTREPLUS

EXPERT QUOTE

We do occasionally get eight-page CVs, but we rarely read all eight pages. However much experience and background you've got, you need to summarize and condense and make it relevant to the job you're applying for. We really don't need to know about jobs done seven or eight years ago. Relevance is the key. Give details of your most relevant experience, even if it isn't from your current job.

DAVID GILES, NATALIE WILSHAW AND PAUL TURNER, HUMAN RESOURCES, WESTLAND HELICOPTERS LTD

7

CVs with special considerations

Some CVs don't have 'problems', as such, but they do require consideration if you are going to make the most of your skills and experience. They include CVs for:

- school or college leavers;

- those returning to work after a career break;

- career changers.

CVs for school, college and university leavers

What do you put in your CV when you have little or no work experience? How can an employer judge your strengths and weaknesses? To some extent, it depends on employers to see potential in an untried applicant. However, you can make things easier for them.

Personal profile

Use this section of your CV to outline your positive features: your strengths, interests and personal qualities. Use it to give an idea of the direction you want your career to take.

Qualifications

At this stage in your career, your qualifications are what you have to offer in place of experience and workplace skills, so cover them in detail.

Achievements

Add a separate key achievements section highlighting successes, duties or responsibilities not covered in your qualifications: heading teams, gaining awards, running special-interest groups or voluntary work, for example.

Work experience

Although you don't have a career history, make the most of what work experience you do have. Even if it's dissimilar to the job you are applying for, any experience will be useful. It shows you are familiar with the working environment and understand the importance of basics such as punctuality, following instructions, getting on with colleagues and taking responsibility.

Include holiday jobs, Saturday jobs, work-experience programmes, voluntary work, work placements and so on.

Transferable skills

Even if you have few specific skills, you can still show that you have a good range of basic competencies. Mine the experience you do have for transferable skills that will establish that you have potential and will readily gain more specific skills through training and experience.

Transferable skills are the skills that underpin every job and they include things like:

- problem solving;

- problem analysis;

- communication skills – written, verbal and interpersonal;

- decision making;

- organizing – planning and prioritizing;

- time and resources management;

- computer and IT skills.

Break down every significant task and responsibility you've undertaken into their underlying transferable skills.

Example

You were responsible for advertising the school music festival, designing and printing fliers for the event, which means you used:

Design and written communication skills, computer and IT skills to produce the fliers; budgeting skills and decision-making skills to decide how and where to print and distribute them; negotiating skills to get the best possible rates and also to persuade local clubs and retailers to take as many as possible; planning and prioritizing skills to schedule when they have to be delivered, printed and distributed to meet a range of deadlines; organizing skills to organize volunteers to cut, fold and deliver fliers to distribution points; interpersonal and communication skills to keep volunteers and distributors on-side.

The key is to take these transferable skills you've used in other situations and fit them to the job you are applying for – understand what underlying skills the job needs and demonstrate that you have them.

Explore all your advantages fully, and keep them in mind when compiling your CV.

Example CV for a school leaver

Name
1 Anystreet
Anytown AA0 0AA
Tel. 00000 000000; Mob. 00000 000000
E-mail: name@anyisp.co.uk

Personal profile
A friendly, outgoing person with good communication skills developed in a variety of voluntary work positions supporting a wide range of ages and abilities. Responsible, conscientious and happy to work both as part of a team and on own initiative having had experience of both.

Achievements
- Representing school in swimming and athletics teams
- Participating in Race for Life 2013
- Secretary of Anytown Under-18 Athletics team
- Elected Team Captain for Inter-Schools tournament.

Education
2008–present: XYZ School
GCSEs
French, English Language, Maths, General Science, Information Technology – grade A, History – grade C
A levels
French A*
English Language B

Voluntary work experience
Working with the elderly
Regularly visited four residents of local sheltered housing scheme to help with shopping and everyday household tasks.
Holiday play scheme
Worked with 7–9-year-olds on a variety of supervised projects from digging a wildlife pond to setting up an ant farm.
Summer sports project
Coached under-11s in squash, badminton and tennis in groups of four or five during summer and Easter holidays.

Personal details
Date of birth: 8 September 1996
Driver with full clean UK driving licence
Non-smoker.

Example CV for a school leaver with relevant experience

Name

1 Anystreet,

Anytown AA0 0AA

Tel. 00000 000000

E-mail: name@anyisp.co.uk

Personal Profile

A friendly, outgoing school leaver with a good general education and experience of a range of retail tasks and responsibilities. Dependable, trustworthy and able to work responsibly with customers. Particularly interested in a career in retail, sales or marketing.

Employment experience

2012–present: ABC Convenience Stores Ltd

Sales Assistant

- Served and assisted customers
- Dealt with enquiries and complaints
- Handled cash
- Administered alcohol, tobacco and lottery tickets according to legislation
- Worked evening shift and covered for sickness and staff absence evenings and weekends.

Summer 2012: DEF Furnishings Ltd

Sales Assistant

- Dealt with enquiries
- Took details of customer orders
- Arranged deliveries
- Maintained display areas.

Qualifications

2007–present: XYZ School

Intermediate GNVQs

Media Studies, Business Studies

GCSEs

English, German, History, Information Technology – grade A, Maths, Economics, Art, General Science – grade B

Computer skills

Familiar with everyday usage including word processing and internet use. Some use of spreadsheets and databases.

Personal details

Date of birth: 16 February 1996

Interests: Clarinet player, member of youth orchestra.

Example CV for a college leaver

Name
1 Anystreet
Anytown AA0 0AA
Tel. 00000 000000
Mobile 00000 000000
E-mail: name@anyisp.co.uk

Personal profile
A highly motivated computer studies student with a recently completed BTEC National Diploma in Computer Science, looking for a position that will provide an opportunity to continue building further experience in this field.

Qualifications
2012–present: XYZ College
BTEC National Diploma in Computer Science
Specializing in
Networking and ICT Support
The course covered all aspects of computing, including:
- computer systems
- communications technology
- computational methods
- software development
- programming practice
- network design and administration.

2005–2012: ABC School
A levels: Information Technology A*, Maths A, Economics B
GCSEs: Seven, including Maths, English and IT

Work experience
2012–present: EFG Stores
Sales Assistant (evenings)
- Served and assisted customers
- Handled cash
- Dealt with enquiries and complaints.

2013–present: XYZ College
Administrative Assistant (part-time)
- Maintained files and records
- Undertook printing and photocopying for members of staff and students
- Carried out routine administrative work.

cont

Personal details

Date of Birth: 9 April 1994

Interests: Reading, swimming, computer gaming

                      Recently designed and set up website for special-interest gamers' group

Full clean UK driving licence.

CVs after a career break

Career breaks happen for a number of reasons. Bringing up children is the most usual one, but there can be others such as looking after elderly parents, travel or other interests, personal development, redundancy or unemployment. Don't underestimate what you have learnt during your break, especially transferable skills. See Chapter 4 for more about the useful skills that most employers value. However, a short course to update your technical skills could be a good idea, especially if you are returning after a few years.

Personal profile

Link the three stages of your career – what you used to do, what you did during your break, and what you intend to do in the future – into a logical whole.

Key skills

Include:

- new skills and experience gained during your break;

- anything you have done to improve or update your skills and qualifications;

- ways you have kept up with developments in your profession;

- positive ways your character has changed – increased maturity, responsibility, understanding, confidence or flexibility, for example.

Career history

Include your break. Be positive about what you have gained, and include relevant duties and responsibilities as you would for any other job. Include any part-time or voluntary work and see the previous section for advice about how to mine this for useful skills.

Example CV for someone returning to work after a career break

Name
1 Anystreet
Anytown AA0 0AA
Tel. 00000 000000
E-mail: name@anyisp.co.uk

Personal profile
An experienced and methodical medical records administrator with an extensive background in the verification, storage and retrieval of records both as documentation and on database, returning to the workforce with updated skills, seeking a position where she can be fully employed.

Key skills
- Currently undertaking NVQ level 4 in Clerical Administration
- Maintaining, developing and administering medical records and data systems
- Collecting, storing and retrieving patient data
- Formulating strategies for handling volume records
- Implementing effective procedures for storing and retrieving
- Supervising staff compiling and inputting record data, and storing documents
- Developing user-friendly methods of staff processing
- Undertaking first-stage statistical analysis
- Preparing and supplying information for staff and departments.

Career history
2009–present
Responsible for the full-time care of my two children, now at school.
- School parent governor
- Fundraiser for the Children's Activity Programme
- Treasurer for local conservation group. Duties included:
  - Bookkeeping
  - Maintaining accounts using Microsoft Excel
  - Preparing books for external auditing.

2002–2009: XYZ Hospital Trust
Records Administrator
Responsible for all aspects of receiving, storing, retrieving and supplying data.
- Supervised staff of 10
- Maintained and updated records and files
- Checked records in and out
- Noted inconsistencies and queried as necessary
- Processed both written documents and computerized records and printouts.

cont

1999–2002: ABC Health Centre
Administrative Assistant
Provided clerical and administrative support to Centre Administrator.
- Maintained and updated records
- Input and retrieved data and statistical information
- Coordinated communications between staff, clinics and clinic users
- Monitored use of consumables.

Education and training
City College
CLAIT
Computer skills
Microsoft Office including Excel, Word, Office Outlook and Explorer
Database and record systems:
- Access database
- D-base 3
- MediTech tailored statistical package.

CVs for career changers

The importance of making your CV relevant has been emphasized throughout this book. Don't leave it to the employer to pick out the key points: put them on page 1 of your CV. You need to know what's relevant in this new situation, so gather all the information you can to make an informed and intelligent application. (See Chapters 1 and 3.) You also need to link the skills and experience you already have to the skills and experience you need for your new job. It's important to make the link yourself and emphasize it in your CV, rather than hope the employer will do it for you.

Personal profile

Use your personal profile to link your previous occupation, the reason for change, and your future career into a logical and convincing story that makes your direction clear.

Key skills

Pick out the skills, qualities and achievements that suit your new career. Include:

- existing skills and experience of value in your new role, including transferable skills that are useful in many jobs;

- new qualifications and skills;

- the personal qualities that make you right for the job.

Career history

Pick out the duties and responsibilities that match your new career, especially transferable or 'soft' skills such as dealing with people, problem solving and decision making. See Chapter 4 for more about these skills which are valued by most employers.

Example CV for a career changer

Name

1 Anystreet

Anytown AA0 0AA

Tel. 00000 000000

Mobile 00000 000000

E-mail: name@anyisp.co.uk

Personal profile

A fully qualified counsellor with direct experience of supporting people from a range of ages and abilities, detailed knowledge of young people in particular, a background in the voluntary sector and extensive experience of working with the public in general.

Key skills

- Certificate of Counselling Practice (AEB)
- Certificate of Counselling Theory (AEB)
- Counselling young people with a variety of problems
- Working alongside Social Services
- Managing a heavy caseload
- Crisis intervention
- Dealing with a wide range of people.

Career history

2012–present: EFG Project

Volunteer Counsellor

Counselled young people with a range of problems centring on homelessness.

- Worked on telephone helpline and conducted one-to-one sessions
- Worked with Social Services implementing general policy as well as working on specific cases
- Gave advice and information about housing and benefit entitlements
- Participated in supervision and support meetings
- Planned and prioritized a full caseload including crisis intervention when necessary.

cont

2009–present: XYZ Transport Ltd

Patient Services Transport Driver

Provided driver support for local ring-and-ride health trust scheme

- Covered two district outpatients departments, three clinics and three day centres
- Collected service users from home, assisted them on and off vehicle and ensured their comfort and safety at all times
- Assisted and supported special needs patients as necessary.

2004–2009: Variable

Delivery Driver

Delivered products to local businesses; maintained full delivery records, schedules and logs.

Education and training

2009–present: XYZ College

Certificate of Counselling Practice (AEB)

Certificate of Counselling Theory (AEB)

1998–2004: ABC School

GCSEs: Seven, including Maths, English and IT.

Personal details

Date of birth:	15 August 1987
Interests:	IT, reading, swimming
Driving licences:	Full clean UK driving licence
	PSV licence

CVs when you already have a CV

If you're in work and already have a CV that successfully got you your current job, I expect you've skipped most of the chapters so far. This section is for you because you still need to update your CV, however. So here are some tips for doing it successfully (because I don't suppose anything I say will make you go back and start again from scratch).

Do not simply insert details of your current job into your old CV; use this as an opportunity to refresh the whole thing:

- Check the entire layout

  - Does it look as good on screen as it does on paper? It's more likely to be seen online now than when you last applied for a job.

- Are the keywords all there? As above, your CV is more likely to be selected via a search app these days. See Chapter 13 for more information about online CVs.

- Does the layout and typeface reflect your current status and professionalism?

- Could the way you express yourself in it be improved upon now?

- Focus attention on you and your current job

  - Update (or add) your personal profile at the top of the page to reflect what you now have to offer

  - Include relevant social media links – to your LinkedIn profile, for example

  - Update (or add) your key skills section and include any relevant training or qualifications you've gained since your previous job

  - Give the most space to your current position and include all relevant details of your duties, responsibilities and achievements

  - Edit the information on previous jobs and cut back severely on anything more than 10 years ago

- Is the story clear?

  - When you look at your CV, does it tell a coherent story about who you are now, where you've come from and where you're going?

  - Where could you strengthen or refine it to tell a clearer story?

  - Can you spot problems that could be dealt with or identify training or experience gaps that could be rectified?

  - Do you like, trust and respect the person you see in your CV?

EXPERT QUOTE

When we were recruiting for a new shopping centre, someone told me she was 'just a housewife' and didn't have any skills. Ten minutes later we'd only just finished listing all the skills she used every day, from planning and organizing to negotiating and persuading.

MARK COLTON, BUSINESS DEVELOPMENT TEAM, JOBCENTREPLUS

8
CVs for specific jobs

Different jobs have different requirements. Some ask for academic or technical qualifications, some call for specific personal qualities, while others demand a track record of achievement. Emphasize your suitability for the job by highlighting the relevant parts of your CV to accentuate these key skills and qualities.

With the advertisement and job description in mind, decide on your most relevant skills and add other competencies you know would be useful. Use the first page for key facts and high-priority information, with back-up details on the second page.

The clerical CV

Office administrators ensure the company runs smoothly, professionally and effectively. Organizations suffer when administration is incompetent, so the key question in the employer's mind is 'Are you efficient?' – meaning, are you:

- well organized?
- competent?
- resourceful?
- proficient?
- capable?
- professional?
- helpful?

When applying for a clerical, secretarial or administrative job, highlight:

- your specific technical skills – the ability to use certain software or equipment;
- your clerical, administrative and organizational skills and experience;
- your experience in relevant areas, such as data handling;
- your proficiency and dependability;
- your ability to work with others.

Focus attention on the following CV sections.

Personal profile

Make yourself sound proficient and professional.

Key skills

Many clerical jobs require specific skills such as word processing, language or book-keeping skills, use of particular software packages, familiarity with equipment or knowledge of a specific process. Review all your skills, matching the job specification and using your knowledge of what the job is likely to require.

Key experience

It's experience that makes people competent and able to keep things running smoothly, so add an extra section highlighting yours.

Include things relevant to many positions such as staff supervision and planning, along with specific experience such as data handling, for example.

Career history

Clerical jobs can be broadly similar, so giving details of duties and responsibilities can appear repetitive. Concentrate on your most recent job and summarize the rest.

Example CV for a clerical job

Name

1 Anystreet

Anytown AA0 0AA

Tel. 00000 000000

E-mail: name@anyisp.co.uk

Personal profile

A senior office administrator and PA with experience of accounts, order office and general office work including management of up to five staff. Punctual, reliable and methodical, good at handling a variety of tasks efficiently, with a strong aptitude for organization and administration.

Key skills

Providing expert and confidential executive support and office management

- Windows XP – Word, Outlook Express, Excel, Access, PowerPoint
- Audio skills including Dictaphone transcription
- Managing junior staff including training and support
- Executive office administration:
  - Diary scheduling
  - Executive-level correspondence
  - Time-sensitive assignments
  - Supply: inventory and purchasing
  - Advanced computer applications.

Key experience

Managing all office activities on a day-to-day basis

- Providing reliability and continuity in office procedures
- Designing and implementing data entry procedures
- Planning and prioritizing workload including secretarial duties, invoicing and purchasing functions
- Purchasing office consumables; researching and purchasing most cost-effective office equipment including photocopier and printers, generating thousands of pounds in savings
- Monitoring printing and stationery costs and implementing cost-effective measures.

Career history

2008 to present: ABC plc

Office Manager/Executive Assistant

Reported directly to senior management; worked independently on a daily basis, and managed comprehensive day-to-day office operations.

- Set up agendas and minuted all departmental meetings up to and including board level
- Organized client preparations and corporate entertainment

cont

- Trained staff in office procedures
- Coordinated department work schedules
- Paid all bills, made bank deposits, tracked invoices and expenses
- Compiled monthly budget reports
- Prepared quantity audits, projections and financial statements
- Maintained computer systems and confidential records
- Created databases, word processing and reports.

2004 to 2008: DEF Ltd
Office Manager

2001 to 2004: GHI & Co
Administrative Assistant

1998 to 2001: JKL Ltd
Department Secretary
Clerical Assistant

Education and training
XYZ Business College
RSA Stage II
RSA Stage III
NCBC Certificate: Finance for Administrators.

Personal details
Date of birth: 24 January 1980
Interests: Aerobics, swimming and walking
Full clean UK driving licence.

The sales and marketing CV

Sales people ensure the company sells its products and makes a profit. The question to keep in mind is 'Can you sell?' Emphasize your past success and highlight your:

- ability to sell;
- successful track record;
- drive and enthusiasm;
- competence and integrity;
- confidence in your abilities.

Concentrate attention on the following key CV sections.

Personal profile

Get your energy, commitment and enthusiasm across.

Key achievements

Include a section that highlights your achievements: your ability to meet and exceed targets, increase turnover and profit, increase orders, win new customers and gain repeat orders from satisfied customers.

Career history

Expand on your success and include your areas of knowledge. Experience other than sales but relevant to the job can be valuable. Buyers like to feel they are dealing with someone who speaks their language.

Example CV for a sales or marketing job

Name
1 Anystreet
Anytown AA0 0AA
Tel. 00000 000000
E-mail: name@anyisp.co.uk

Personal profile
A highly motivated sales executive with more than eight years' experience in all aspects of market development and regional sales management and a successful background in business turnaround, with the proven ability to develop specialized marketing strategies. Effective at motivating others to achieve individual and organizational goals with successful sales methods and training procedures.

Key achievements
- Revitalized two new neglected ranges, increasing profit by 200 per cent
- Established new product range, taking it from conception to completion and achieving £150,000 turnover in first year with 25 per cent annual growth thereafter
- Increased technical support service uptake by 85 per cent
- Organized ongoing programmes for sales personnel with training in sales and product knowledge, thereby decreasing staff turnover by 37 per cent and increasing met targets by 57 per cent
- Planned and organized nationwide programme of exhibitions

cont

- Prepared and delivered presentations at all levels, including hands-on product demonstrations to groups of all sizes.

Career history

2010 to present: ABC Systems Ltd

Regional Manager

Responsible for seven retail operations

- Increased overall profits by 75 per cent
- Consistently exceeded targets
- Raised profile and increased enquiries by 25 per cent
- Increased sales by 45 per cent overall
- Monitored sales statistics and controlled stock levels and ordering
- Assessed and trained staff.

2006 to 2010: DEF Ltd

Sales Manager

Responsible for own territory plus sales team of five

- Increased overall profits by 7–15 per cent
- Consistently met and exceeded personal sales targets
- Undertook staff reviews and training.

2003 to 2006: ABC Systems Ltd

Sales Executive

- Developed virgin territory
- Exceeded target performance by 15 per cent
- Planned marketing campaigns for sales promotions
- Achieved 40 per cent increase in enquiries at peak of promotion.

1999 to 2003: Various

Retail Sales

Telesales

Education and training

XYZ University

BSc (Hons) 2.2 Economics.

Personal details

Date of Birth: 2 October 1977

Interests: Badminton and squash

                    Riding

Full clean UK driving licence

Non-smoker

References available on request.

CVs for technical jobs

Technical staff carry out complex production processes competently, accurately and knowledgeably. As they often know most about the process, they are usually problem solvers as well.

An employer needs to know you have the technical proficiency – the knowledge and experience – to take over smoothly and efficiently with as little disruption to production as possible. The question they will be asking is 'Can you do the job?'

Highlight your:

- specific technical skills;
- qualifications;
- experience in specific areas;
- dependability;
- accuracy;
- methodical approach;
- organizational skills;
- ability to work as part of a team.

Make full use of the following CV sections.

Personal profile

Emphasize your proficiency.

Key qualifications

Qualifications are important in technical jobs. Add a section highlighting your qualifications and training as well as the usual education and training section.

Key skills

Your technical skills are vital, along with your knowledge and experience, so spell them out.

Example CV for a technical job

Name
1 Anystreet
Anytown AA0 0AA
Tel. 00000 000000
E-mail: name@anyisp.co.uk

Personal profile

An extremely thorough, methodical research assistant with experience of obtaining, collecting and analysing biological data, and a specific interest in molecular biology, especially cell signalling systems.

Key qualifications
- MSc Molecular Biology
- BSc Biochemistry.

Key skills
- Knowledge of PCR, SSCP, SDS, PAGE and blotting techniques
- Background in cellular and molecular haematology
- Understanding of human molecular biology
- Experience in haematological cell signalling
- Coordinating, planning and running experiments
- Analysing data.

Career history

2010–present: ABC Centre for Research

Laboratory Assistant

Conducted research into mitogen-activated protein kinase phosphorylation in acute myoblastic leukaemic cells:
- Designed and organized experiments with aim of acquiring specific research data
- Undertook experimental procedures
- Collected and collated results
- Analysed preliminary data by computer
- Prepared preliminary report on findings.

2006–2007: DEF University

Research Assistant

Research assistant to Professor of Oncology, investigating the molecular characteristics predictive of clinical outcomes in patients with myeloblastic leukaemia.

cont

Education and training

2001–2006: DEF University

MSc Molecular Biology

BSc Biochemistry (2.1)

1994–2001: XYZ School

A levels: Biology, Chemistry, Maths

GCSEs: Nine including Maths and English.

Personal details

Date of birth: 11 June 1983

Interests: Swimming and sailing

Full clean UK driving licence

Non-smoker.

The management CV

Managers make sure that everything happens according to plan. They ensure that everybody else works effectively and efficiently, and if there is a problem, they find out what the trouble is, devise a solution and implement it. The key question for managers is 'Will you get results?' Demonstrate you know how to:

- organize and run a department;

- develop, inspire, lead and support a team;

- motivate people;

- develop the potential in staff members;

- devise and implement strategy;

- make decisions and solve problems;

- manage change successfully.

Concentrate on the following aspects of your CV.

Personal profile

Highlight your managerial abilities.

Key skills

As well as specific technical skills, think about transferable management skills such as:

- **analytical skills:** the ability to weigh up facts and make appropriate judgements and decisions;
- **problem-solving skills:** the ability to weigh problems, assess options and arrive at a solution;
- **communication skills:** the ability to receive and convey information at different levels;
- **interpersonal skills:** the ability to motivate, influence and persuade people.

Key achievements

Show that you have achieved results in the past. Include a section giving your key achievements and showing your track record of success.

Career history

Your experience counts. Few people go straight into management from college or university, and your foundation in business is important. Detail your duties and responsibilities.

Example CV for a management job

Name
1 Anystreet
Anytown AA0 0AA
Tel. 00000 000000
E-mail: name@anyisp.co.uk

Personal profile
A sales manager with 6 years' experience in computer systems, currently responsible for introducing leading US interactive software to the European market. Proficient in personnel recruitment and effective team management with comprehensive skills in strategic planning and implementation.

cont

Key skills

- Computer sales – hardware, software and peripherals, interactive systems
- UK and European sales
- Eastern European market and culture
- Recruitment and training of sales and technical staff
- High-level negotiation with major clients
- Working in new and growing markets
- Fluent business German.

Key achievements

- Managing a team that increased European sales by 27 per cent over three years
- Increasing regional UK sales from £70 million to £120 million through training and motivating staff
- Introducing new interactive software, resulting in an initial 43 per cent sales increase and a growth rate of 14 per cent annually
- Recruiting and training sales and technical staff for Europe with the emphasis on the growing Eastern European market
- Leading, training and motivating a pioneering East German sales team, raising market share from 0 per cent to 12 per cent within 18 months
- Maintaining steady sales of original lines
- Elected 'Manager of the Year' 2011 by the Professional Management Association.

Career history

2010–present: ABC Software Ltd
Commercial Operations Manager, Europe
Managed £240 million sales operation selling and marketing new interactive software products, responsible for all commercial and logistical operations in Europe

- Full responsibility for sales and marketing
- Recruited and trained technical sales personnel
- Liaised with distributors in 14 regions in East and West Europe
- Negotiated suitable warehousing sites with authorities and property agents in each region.

2003–2010: DEF Ltd
Regional Manager
Managed £120 million UK sales operation, responsible for all sales and marketing operations in UK

- Responsible for recruiting and training sales team to the highest level in a technically demanding field
- Increased Southern Region profits by 15 per cent over two years
- Contracted out after-sales service to reduce overheads
- Negotiated additional technical back-up facilities for improved client service and increased client retention.

cont

Sales Manager
- Set team sales budgets, assigned territories and targets
- Undertook staff reviews and training
- Consistently met and exceeded personal sales targets
- Gained MBA 2005
- Promoted to Regional Manager 2006.

1999–2003: GHI Ltd
Sales Representative
- Exceeded target performance by 17 per cent
- Achieved Top Ten National Sales Award and Top Regional Sales Award.

Education and training
XYZ University: **BA (Hons) 2.2 Economics**
UVW Business School: **MBA**

Computer training:
Microsoft Word, Excel, Lotus, Windows XP, planning and presentation software, internet and e-mail
Expertise in all ABC Software products.

Personal details
Date of birth: 18 November 1976
Interests: Entered London Marathon 2011–2014
Full clean UK and European driving licence.

CVs for creative jobs

Creative people are problem solvers and solution providers. They use their skill and talent to achieve results with originality and flair. Employers need to know you will do that to a deadline and on budget, or their business will suffer. The question they are asking is 'Will you deliver?' Your CV needs to highlight your:

- thorough understanding of your field;

- track record of effective, innovative and creative solutions;

- ability to come up with results every time;

- drive and ambition to continue to produce top-quality work;

- ability to work both individually and as part of a team to get results.

Focus on the following aspects of your CV.

Personal profile

Present yourself as innovative yet businesslike.

Key skills

Practical ability and technical competence are important. Good foundation skills ensure that style and originality can be attained every time.

Key achievements

Creative jobs are result-oriented. Include a section outlining your successes: work that fulfilled its creative brief inventively, to deadline and within budget, and that actively contributed to the company's success.

Career history

Your experience is important: the creative and practical challenges you have faced, how you have overcome them, and the skill and knowledge you have developed as a result.

Example CV for a creative job

Name
1 Anystreet
Anytown AA0 0AA
Tel. 00000 000000
E-mail: name@anyisp.co.uk

Personal profile
An innovative and intelligent exhibition designer with a sound understanding of 3D design and presentation and a background in delivering a comprehensive display design service for both local authority and private clients.

Key skills
- Computer design software
- Design, specification, planning and budgeting
- Liaising with internal and external clients and contractors

cont

- Supervising construction, layout and finish
- Working with a team to produce a distinctive 'brand feel'.

Key achievements

- Successful design and planning of more than a dozen feature exhibitions
- Devising an innovative and foolproof 'pack and show' display system which allows exhibitions to be toured to schools safely and attractively
- Designing, specifying and supervising interior renovation of museum annex to give café space and overspill area
- Bringing projects in on time and to budget, contributing to the success of the museum.

Career history

2010–present: ABC Museum

Exhibition Designer

Inclusive renovation of museum galleries, having responsibility for:

- Assessing requirements for exhibition and liaising with curators and experts to achieve the desired results
- Design and implementation
- Planning and budgeting
- Materials specification and purchasing
- Managing construction team and local contractors.

2003–2010: DEF Ltd

Chief Display Designer

Display Designer

Designed and built in-store displays, promotions and window dressing as part of display team for major city-centre department store. As Chief Display Designer, personally responsible for managing display team and designing main windows for key merchandise.

Education and training

1999–2003: XYZ College of Art

Foundation Diploma in Art and Design

BA (Hons) 3D Design

Personal details

Date of birth: 8 December 1978

Interests: Member of local archaeological society

                    Member of local history society

Full clean UK driving licence.

CVs for practical jobs

Practical jobs keep companies running smoothly, and involve maintenance, warehousing, deliveries, security and so on. If these jobs are not done reliably, other employees can't do their own work, the company becomes inefficient and productivity drops.

Companies need competent, dependable people who work accurately, effectively and efficiently. The key question is 'Are you reliable?' Highlight your:

- practical skills and abilities;

- qualifications and training such as NVQ and City & Guilds;

- hands-on experience;

- competence and reliability;

- self-reliance along with the ability to follow instructions;

- flexibility and adaptability.

Demonstrate your suitability in the following CV sections.

Personal profile

Highlight your competence and reliability.

Key skills

Concentrate on your practical skills. Show you understand what the job requires and that you have the right skills and experience. Include relevant qualifications and training.

Career history

Experience is important in practical jobs. Focus on the tasks and responsibilities of each job and the knowledge and competence you gained.

Example CV for a practical job

Name

1 Anystreet

Anytown AA0 0AA

Tel. 00000 000000

E-mail: name@anyisp.co.uk

Personal profile

A trained, professional, highly competent electrician, experienced in all types of electrical work including domestic, commercial, industrial, electrical construction and estimating.

Key skills

- City & Guilds Electrical Installation Certificate
- New home construction wiring
- Repair and maintenance of electrical equipment
- Wiring for building conversions, renovations and extensions
- Wiring for offices and manufacturing businesses
- Implementation of health and safety legislation.

Career history

2010–present: ABC Electric

Chief Electrician

Foreman working with crews of 2 to 12 on medium-sized projects including complete wiring of business and manufacturing businesses and new home construction.

- Scheduled and supervised work
- Checked quality and productivity
- Provided layouts
- Responsible for:
    - Estimates
    - Work schedules
    - Billing
    - Ordering parts and equipment
    - Maintaining inventories
    - Customer service.

2006–2010: DEF Construction Ltd

Electrician

Worked on a variety of commercial and industrial projects such as hospitals and high-rise buildings where safety and reliability were highly important.

cont

2002–2006: GHJ Construction Ltd
Electrician
Team member on construction of XYZ Shopping Mall in Anytown.

Education and training
2000–2002: ABC College
City & Guilds Electrical Installation Certificate.

Personal details
Date of birth: 1 June 1984
Interests: Jazz and music in general
                   Fell walking – member of local walking and climbing group

Full clean UK driving licence
Non-smoker
References available on request.

CVs for customer relations jobs

The main focus of customer relations is dealing with people: making sales, dealing with complaints, answering enquiries, or offering help and advice, face to face or over the phone. The key question the employer has to ask is 'Are you customer-focused?'
Highlight your:

- experience of dealing with people;
- positive approach to customer service;
- interpersonal and communication skills;
- influencing and persuading skills;
- ability to stay calm under pressure.

Personal profile

Sound friendly, helpful and dependable.

Key skills

Include the skills that make you good at dealing with people and a first-class interface between the company and the public. Include relevant technical skills.

Key experience

Include a section outlining your experience of dealing with people.

Career history

Focus on the duties and responsibilities relevant to customer service.

Example CV for a job in customer relations

Name
1 Anystreet
Anytown AA0 0AA
Tel. 00000 000000
E-mail: name@anyisp.co.uk

Personal profile
An experienced travel consultant with a pleasant, friendly manner, a genuine interest in people and a strong desire to provide clients with the best possible holiday experience.

Key skills
- Patient and tactful with good listening skills
- Excellent interpersonal skills – face to face, over the phone and via e-mail
- Remaining calm and organized in a pressured environment
- Smart appearance
- Continual updating of product knowledge and personal skills
- Fast, accurate keyboard skills and good general IT skills
- First-rate knowledge of travel geography, travel requirements, health requirements, passports, visas and other travel documents.

Key experience
- Four years' experience as a consultant dealing with both the general public and business travellers
- Handling enquiries and giving information
- Helping and advising on options and choices
- Handling problems, queries and complaints efficiently and effectively.

cont

Career history

2010–present: ABC Travel

Travel Consultant

Work as part of team dealing with customer queries and bookings – package, fly-drive and specialist holidays as well as business travel

- Advise on suitable destinations, routes, methods of travel and other options, depending on client need and expectation
- Assisted business travellers with information and advice, frequently making and confirming bookings at short notice and to tight deadlines
- Advised on necessary travel documents, health requirements, etc
- Checked and verified flight and accommodation availability, timings, budget requirements, car hire, trips and excursions
- Handled cash and credit card transactions efficiently, including cancellations and changed bookings
- Consistently met, and regularly exceeded, company targets.

Education and training

BTEC National Diploma in Travel and Tourism

The course covered all aspects of travel and tourism, including

- Worldwide travel geography
- Airport operations
- Resort representatives
- Finance
- Travel services.

Language skills

- French
- Spanish.

Computer skills

- Windows XP
- Standard business software
- Travel industry standard software.

Personal details

Date of birth: 19 September 1990

Interests: Art and antiques; watercolour painting

Member of local drama society

Full clean UK driving licence

Non-smoker.

EXPERT QUOTE

The job description will ask for exactly what we want. Include as many of the Essentials and Desirables as you can. If you haven't got a particular item, include something similar, or something from outside work. Often, all shortlisted candidates have the Essentials and selection depends on those Desirable requirements.

MAGGIE FELLOWS, PROJECT MANAGER, SOUTH WEST TUC

EXPERT QUOTE

We look for competencies and for candidates to provide evidence of what they've actually done. As long as it's current evidence it doesn't have to be work based, it can be from any area of life.

ROBERT JOHNSON, AREA DIRECTOR, ACAS SOUTH WEST

EXPERT QUOTE

When we're recruiting, we often have to read 50 or 60 CVs at a time. You just can't do that in any great detail, so make it easy – bring the relevant information to the fore so that it's practically shouting out to be picked.

DAVID GILES, NATALIE WILSHAW AND PAUL TURNER, HUMAN RESOURCES, WESTLAND HELICOPTERS LTD

EXPERT QUOTE

Don't send a blanket CV, target it to the job you're applying for. It's a bit like a sales pitch, say why they should pick you out of all the other candidates. What can you do for them? What are the benefits of employing you?

DEBBIE MACEKE, RESOURCE CENTRE MANAGER, ROLLS-ROYCE

9
Application forms

Some organizations prefer to use a standard application form rather than receive CVs. There are several reasons for this:

- The standard format allows quick screening.

- It's easier to see if candidates have key requirements.

- Inconsistencies and omissions show up.

- Only serious applicants go to the trouble of completing them; it's easier to send a CV than to sit down and fill out a lengthy form.

Some also believe application forms are fairer, not favouring people who simply write a good CV.

Take the time to complete any application form properly. Use your CV for information and inspiration. Before you start:

- Read the application form through and note any instructions such as 'list most recent jobs first' or 'use block capitals'.

- If the form is on paper, take a photocopy to fill out, correct and amend first.

- Complete online forms offline – where possible – copy and paste into Word so you can check spelling and grammar, get someone else to proof-read it, and so on. Saving what you've done offline also means that it's there for you to use again whenever you need to.

- If you *are* completing the form online (some sites don't allow you to copy and paste), make use of any facility to save the form and return to it in your own time so that you don't feel pressured to fill it all in at once.

- Application forms are often sent out with an information pack, so have the job description, your CV and any other information to hand.

- Fill in every section, don't leave spaces. If something is not relevant to you, put 'not applicable' in that box.

- If you continue onto a separate sheet of paper, put your name and address at the top, along with the job you are applying for and any reference number in case it gets detached.

- Never put 'see attached CV'. The purpose of application forms is to standardize information, so asking the employer to read your CV is pointless.

- Take a copy of your finished form to refer to when you are called for interview.

Application forms section by section

Most forms have the following sections:

- personal details;
- educational details;
- employment record;
- job requirements;
- personal statement;
- references;
- declaration.

Personal details

This asks for your name, address and contact details. It can also ask for:

- details of your driving licence;
- whether you require a work permit;
- whether you have any criminal convictions;
- details of your leisure interests.

If you are asked specifically for a full clean driving licence and you have penalty points, you must declare them. If you don't have a full licence but do have a provisional one, it's worth putting that down.

If a work permit or any other document is required, send a photocopy – not the original – with the application form.

If you have a current criminal conviction, write the full details on a separate sheet and send it in a sealed envelope attached to the application form.

If the form asks you for your leisure interests, keep them relevant and interesting. See the 'Personal details' section in Chapter 5, 'Your CV', for more information.

Educational details

This section asks for details of your education and training:

- the school, college and/or university where you studied;

- the dates you were there;

- type of study, full or part time;

- the subject or name of the course;

- the qualifications you obtained.

Don't go back further than your secondary school, and include any training you have done since leaving full-time education. This can be more relevant than your A levels and GCSEs.

Employment record

Starting with your current position, state your employer's name and address, the dates you've worked there, your job title, and most importantly, a brief description of your main duties and responsibilities. Treat this section as you would the career history on your CV, and make your duties and responsibilities relevant to the job you are applying for.

Don't leave unexplained gaps. Put down something even if you weren't in paid employment: a gap year travelling, bringing up children or whatever.

The form can also ask for reasons for leaving, something you don't have to consider on your CV. Make your reasons positive. Focus on what you were going to, rather than what you were leaving behind. If, for example, you left a job because you were bored and the prospects were poor, turn it around: you wanted a better job where there was more challenge and responsibility and a greater prospect of promotion.

Figure 9.1 gives an example.

FIGURE 9.1 Employment record section of an application form

Dates: from–to	Employer's name and address	Job title and brief description of duties and responsibilities	Reason for leaving
1999–present	XYZ Ltd Anyroad Anytown	Area Sales Manager Planned area forecasts; developed accounts; managed area budget; prioritized schedules; trained sales team	Challenge and improved prospects of working for a high-profile company

You may be asked for your salary details. Include everything that could be classed as salary, for example £XX,XXX pa+bonus, commission, overtime, weighting allowance, etc.

Job requirements

Increasingly, there's a section that lists essential job requirements and asks you to describe briefly how you meet each one. State your experience and add any achievements that demonstrate your competence. Put something against each requirement. A blank space here can mean rejection at the scanning stage.

Figuer 9.2 gives an example.

FIGURE 9.2 Sample 'job requirements' section of an application form

Describe briefly how you meet each of the following job requirements. Continue on a separate sheet of paper if required.	
Team leadership and motivation	Three years as team leader leading team of 6–8 Headed award-winning team (Utrex 2002) Motivated team to exceed target by 15% Introduced motivational bonus scheme, reducing staff turnover by 20%
Designing and delivering training programmes	Trained 350 staff in total over 3 years Designed and delivered programme taking staff from induction to job-ready in 2 weeks Devised rolling product-update programme
Knowledge of NVQ competency framework	Took 50 staff members through NVQ levels 2–4

Alternatively, you could be asked about times you've demonstrated the key skills and personal qualities needed to carry out the job. This could be, 'Use the space provided to describe a time you had to work with others under pressure to achieve a goal', or 'Describe a situation in which you had to deal with a complaint from a member of the public', for example.

To ensure that your answer is comprehensive and well structured, follow the STAR method of compiling the facts:

- **Situation**: what was it, how did it arise, what was your involvement with it?

- **Task**: what was your objective? There could be more than one and they could be conflicting. Serving an unexpected coach party on a tight schedule *and* keeping regular customers happy and well-attended to at the same time, for example.

- **Actions**: what actions did you take to help achieve a favourable outcome?

- **Result**: what was it? Were there any obstacles along the way and how did you overcome them? Why was it a good outcome?

Keep your answers as relevant as possible to the job you're applying for. Look for examples that show you working as part of a team as well as showing individual initiative in situations that have a positive outcome. If you can demonstrate using valued abilities such as interpersonal skills, planning and organizing skills, or can demonstrate your integrity, positivity or adaptability, for example, at the same time, even better!

Personal statement

This is the blank page that asks if you have any additional information to support your application.

An astonishing number of these are left empty, yet this is your opportunity to highlight your relevant skills and achievements and underline your suitability for the job. Include details of your:

- key skills and experience;

- suitability for the job;

- relevant achievements;

- relevant experience and skills gained outside the workplace;

- reasons for applying for the job.

Take each point in the job description and match it to your own skills and experience. See Chapter 2 for more detailed information about matching your skills to the job requirements.

Table 9.1 gives an example.

TABLE 9.1 Matching skills and achievements to job requirements

They want	I have
At least 2 years' secretarial experience	3 years' secretarial experience+2 years' clerical
Good linguist – French or German	C&G Bilingual Secretarial Diploma, French/English. Worked as shipping clerk for French import company
Advanced knowledge of Microsoft Office	MS Word, Access, PowerPoint, Outlook Express
Great keyboard skills	70 wpm + audio typing skills

Turn your notes into a readable statement, adding relevant details:

> *I am currently working as PA to a head of department and have three years'*
> *secretarial experience in this post. My French language skills are excellent,*
> *since I have taken a City & Guilds Bilingual Secretarial Diploma (French/English)*
> *and also worked as shipping clerk for a French import company (XYZ Ltd) for*
> *two years, working for a French manager, handling phone calls in French and*
> *liaising between French and English clients...*

Think about why you are applying for the job. Look forward, not backward: what does this new job offer? Reasons might include:

- increased challenge;
- increased responsibility;
- greater opportunity for development or promotion;
- chance to use specific skills;
- reputation of company;
- career progression.

For example:

> *... (my current job) has given me the opportunity to develop my bookkeeping*
> *skills over the past year. I now find this side of the job more appealing and I am*
> *looking for a position where I can develop my skills more fully. I believe this job*
> *offers just such an opportunity, along with greater responsibility and the chance to*
> *work closely with a small and dedicated team.*

References

Application forms often ask for references, but they are not usually taken up unless a job offer is made. They normally ask for one from your present employer together with a personal reference from a friend or colleague. Give the information, but if you don't want your current employer contacted until you have had an offer, write this on the form.

Declaration

This is the final section. It asks you to declare that the information you have included is true and accurate, and that you have not withheld anything that might affect your application. It asks for your signature and the date.

Remember to sign. Some people are so impatient to finish they forget this last, important detail.

If a job is offered on the basis of anything false or misleading, the offer can be withdrawn. Companies can and will do this, so stick to the truth.

Send your completed form with a covering letter briefly outlining the key points. (See more about this in the next chapter.) Unless a return envelope is provided, send it in a plain white A4 envelope, in good time for the closing date.

EXPERT QUOTE

Use that blank page. Don't be afraid to use headings and bullet points to get your skills across. A good way to organize the information and know you've covered everything is to use the Essentials and Desirables from the job description as headings and say how you fulfil each requirement.

MAGGIE FELLOWS, PROJECT MANAGER, SOUTH WEST TUC

10
Covering letters

Always send a letter with your CV. It's an opportunity to headline your key points and highlight your suitability for the job. A letter that makes a good first impression ensures your CV will be read with just that little bit more interest and attention.

As with CVs, letters must be short, succinct and relevant. They should look professional and be easy to read, which means paying attention to:

- appearance;
- layout;
- readability;
- content.

Appearance

- Use plain, unlined white or cream A4 paper, preferably 100 gsm weight.
- Use one side of the paper only.
- Print it in a style and typeface that match your CV, unless a handwritten letter is specifically asked for.
- Check and double-check grammar and spelling.
- Print the letter out afresh each time you apply for a job. Never send a photocopy.

Layout

Use a standard business layout like the one shown.

Example letter

1 Yourstreet
Yourtown
Yourcounty AA0 0AA
Tel. 00000 000000
Mobile: 00000 000000
E-mail: name@anyisp.co.uk

1 January 2015

Name of recipient
His or her job title
Company name
Company address
Company address AA0 0AA

Re: Recruitment Manager Ref 34 WT

Dear Ms Smith

Write the main body of your letter here _____

_____

_____

_____

_____

_____

_____

_____

_____

_____

_____

_____

_____

Yours sincerely

Your signature

Your full name

Readability

- Keep to one page. Only exceptional covering letters need be longer.

- Keep sentences and paragraphs short. Two short paragraphs are better than one long one. Dense blocks of text are hard to read.

- Make the main points clear. Covering letters are skimmed through rather than read. Even though it's a letter, use bullet points to emphasize your:
  - specific skills;
  - main achievements;
  - key career details.

- Include white space to make it look easy to read and inviting. Use wide margins and paragraph breaks.

- Use a plain, clear 11- or 12-point typeface.

Content

- Write to a named individual, not 'Dear Sir or Madam'.

- Write clearly and concisely.

- Use normal business English. Avoid jargon such as 'with regard to' and 'in respect of'.

- Be positive and enthusiastic. Avoid words like might, maybe, wishing, hoping.

- Customize each covering letter and relate it to the job you are applying for.

What goes into the letter?

Think of covering letters as having four distinct parts.

Paragraph one

Say why you are writing. If it's in reply to an advertised vacancy, include the title of the job you are applying for and where you saw the advertisement. If it's a speculative letter (see Chapter 14, 'Job search strategies'), start with a brief paragraph giving your reason for writing. Make it topical and relevant. For example:

- I am writing to apply for the position of Personal Assistant as advertised in today's *Evening Post.*

- **Ref: 16K Project Manager.** I am writing to apply for the above post as advertised in this month's issue of *Engineering Times*.

- I read with interest of your company's plans to open a new branch in Anytown in yesterday's *Evening Chronicle*.

- Congratulations on securing the new XYZ account as reported in this month's *Gazette.*

- I read with interest on the current *Engineering Today* website about your new contract to manufacture XYZ engineering systems.

- It was really nice to meet you at the recent Business Today exhibition and hear about the recent developments at your company.

Paragraph two

This is the persuasive part that tells them what you can contribute to the company. Include your relevant skills, experience and achievements. If this is a speculative letter (see Chapter 14), mention the sort of job you are interested in. You can split this section into two or three short paragraphs if it makes it easier to read. For example:

- I have been IT Manager at XYZ Ltd for three years and have experience of large-scale software changeover, having restructured the finance department during that time. The problems I've effectively handled include:
  - maintaining turn-around rate during departmental change;
  - designing effective training manuals;
  - taking staff successfully through the change process.

- As you will see from my CV, I have worked on an extensive range of accounts including consumer, recruitment and financial. I have wide experience of creating exciting and imaginative publicity campaigns. Of particular interest to you will be the XYZ campaign, a copy of which I enclose. This prompted a response rate of 22 per cent, the highest ever achieved by the agency.

- Among the skills that will be of most interest to you are:
  - excellent staff management;
  - a first-rate record in administration;
  - proficiency at prioritizing workloads;
  - the ability to implement standard procedures efficiently.

- My recent achievements include organizing and supervising staff training to introduce Microsoft Office as standard across the board. This resulted in a significant increase in both departmental and interdepartmental efficiency.

Paragraph three

Give your reason for applying for the job. Make it positive and persuasive, emphasizing what you can bring to a new position, rather than what you hope the company will do for you. For example:

- I am presently working at the marketing organization XYZ. However, I would very much like to return to production, where I feel my skills and experience could be used more effectively, and would welcome the opportunity this position offers to do so.

- I have enjoyed working at XYZ, and have welcomed the chance this has given me to cultivate my administrative skills. However, I am now looking for a post with more responsibility, and feel that your advertisement offers the opportunity I am looking for.

- I am keen to find an organization offering continued training and development, and the chance to progress in this area. I am therefore very interested in the vacancy you have to offer.

Paragraph four

This should be a short paragraph to close the letter, confirming your interest in the job. For example:

- I would welcome the opportunity to discuss my application with you further, and look forward to hearing from you.

- I would be very happy to discuss my application with you in more detail, and look forward to hearing from you.

- I would really appreciate the opportunity of a short meeting to discuss possible openings within your organization, and will contact your office within the next few days to request a convenient date and time.

Example letter answering an advertised vacancy

1 Yourstreet

Yourtown

Yourcounty AA0 0AA

Tel. 00000 000000

Mobile: 00000 000000

E-mail: name@anyisp.co.uk

1 January 2015

Jane Smith

Personnel Manager

XYZ Ltd

111 Anystreet

Anytown AA0 0AA

Re: Marketing Manager Ref 34 WT

Dear Ms Smith

I am writing to apply for the position of Marketing Manager as advertised in this month's *Retail Direct*.

As you will see from my CV, I have extensive marketing experience, including three years with ABC Ltd. I have a particular interest in product planning, and have successfully researched the market possibilities for several profitable new product lines.

I am at present working for DEF & Co, the product research organization. I would, however, prefer to return to consumer marketing as I believe this is where my skills can be used most effectively. I am consequently very interested in the opportunity your vacancy offers.

I would be very happy to discuss my application with you in more detail, and look forward to hearing from you in the near future.

Yours sincerely

J. Brown

John Brown

Example speculative letter

1 Yourstreet
Yourtown
Yourcounty AA0 0AA
Tel. 00000 000000
Mobile: 00000 000000
E-mail: name@anyisp.co.uk

1 January 2015

Jane Smith
Senior Staff Coordinator
XYZ Training Ltd
111 Anystreet
Anytown AA0 0AA

Dear Ms Smith

I was interested to read of the new education initiatives for the area outlined in today's *Evening Post*, and wonder if you have an opening for an adult literacy and numeracy teacher with counselling qualifications.

As you will see from my CV, I have considerable experience of working with people from a variety of backgrounds. I have been involved with the adult literacy scheme at the ABC Centre since its opening in 2012, as a tutor and student adviser, and I also work as a volunteer counsellor with the DEF Trust.

I have City & Guilds qualifications in both Basic Education Teaching and Practical Counselling. In addition, I have attended GHI College's Planned Adult Literacy Course and undergone counselling training with DEF Trust.

As the current project at the ABC Centre is drawing to a close, I am eager to continue to develop my career and make full use of my skills and experience where they would be of value. I believe your organization could offer the opportunity to do so.

I would really appreciate the chance to discuss any suitable positions with you in more detail, and look forward to hearing from you in the near future.

Yours sincerely

J. Brown

John Brown

E-mail

Don't be tempted to be casual because e-mail feels more spontaneous and immediate. A covering letter needs careful thought, however it's delivered. Take the same care that you would with any other:

- Think about what you want to say and how to say it.
- Check spelling and grammar.
- Send letters individually and resist the temptation to copy them to a dozen other people at the same time.
- Present it as well as you would any other letter.

Your name, e-mail address and the date are already at the top of the page. Start your message after this rather than taking up space with further contact details. If you want to include them, put them at the end.

Fill in the subject line – it's an additional opportunity to catch the reader's attention and include valuable keywords. Don't go for a hard sell, though: keep the message clear and professional. Include any job title and reference number. For example:

Subject: Field Sales Manager – CeMAP qualified

Subject: 7 years' Java, LINUX & C++ experience

Subject: Export Exec – China and Asia experience

Make sure your key points appear on the opening screen and give the reader good reasons to scroll down further.

Example e-mail application letter

To: jsmith@abcltd.com

Cc:

Subject: Ref K121 Sales Manager – IT experienced applicant

Dear Ms Smith

I would like to apply for the position of Senior Sales Manager as detailed on salesjobs.com.

My achievements include:

- responsibility for three multi-million pound projects
- increasing XYZ's penetration of the IT sector by 25 per cent
- increasing XYZ's profits by 11 per cent
- increasing the market share of DEF by 15 per cent.

I have an excellent track record in Sales Management, particularly in Information Technology, having worked for some of the major companies in this field.
....(end of opening screen)
As well as being a skilled communicator, supportive, thorough, innovative and decisive, I also possess practical management skills, having:

- led professional teams on major marketing projects
- taken overall responsibility for four major product launches
- formulated policy at all stages of sales development.

I look forward to discussing my application with you in more detail, and I hope to hear from you in the near future. My full CV is attached.

Yours sincerely

Jane Brown

Tel: 00000 000000

If you have a good job advertisement or job description to work from, the letter practically writes itself. All you need to do is confirm that you have what they are asking for.

PERSONAL ASSISTANT

A small city-based environmental charity requires an experienced, mature assistant to provide administrative and secretarial support. Must have excellent organizational abilities and keyboard skills – Microsoft Office Suite currently used. Good communication skills and a confident telephone manner essential as will be dealing with enquiries from the public. Knowledge of bookkeeping and familiarity with spreadsheets would be an advantage, but training will be given to the right applicant. Understanding of environmental issues desirable. Must be able to work on own initiative without supervision.

As in Chapter 3, in the section on using an advertisement to improve your CV, pick out the key requirements from the ad or description then match your own skills and experience to their needs.

They want:	I have:
Administrative and secretarial experience	Currently work as administrative assistant
Maturity – either in age or attitude	Have been in responsible role in admin for over 3 years
The ability to organize	Organize office admin – daily running, meetings, appointments
Ability to work on own initiative without supervision	Prioritize and organize workload currently, required to deal with everyday situations on own initiative and be self-motivated
Computer skills – preferably Microsoft Office	Use Microsoft Word and Outlook at work; Excel for History Society accounts
Good communication skills	Liaise with colleagues and other departments, previously worked in retail dealing with public – answering enquiries and offering help and advice
Confident telephone manner	Deal with calls and enquiries to the department
They would prefer:	
Some bookkeeping experience	Treasurer for Local History Society
Familiarity with spreadsheets	As above
Experience of dealing with the public	As above
Understanding of and sympathy with environmental issues	Reason for interest in job – keen interest in environmental issues and active Member of the Woodland Conservation Volunteer Trust

Once you have a clear idea of how you match the company's requirements, the covering letter practically writes itself. Just take the information and organize it into a readable form:

1 Yourstreet
Yourtown
Yourcounty AA0 0AA
Tel. 00000 000000
Mobile: 00000 000000
e-mail: name@anyisp.co.uk

1 March 2015
Jane Smith
Personnel Manager
XYZ Trust
111 Anystreet
Anytown AA0 0AA

Dear Ms Smith

I am writing to apply for the position of Personal Assistant as advertised in this week's *Daily Advertiser*.

I am currently working as the administrative assistant for ABC Ltd and have been in this responsible job for over three years.

As you will see from my enclosed CV, my responsibilities include organizing the everyday running of the office including word processing letters and reports, dealing with incoming queries, planning and organizing meetings, scheduling appointments, and liaising with colleagues to ensure the smooth running of the department. I currently prioritize and organize my own workload, and am required to deal with everyday situations on my own initiative and be self-motivated.

I have excellent computer skills – I use Microsoft Word and Outlook Express in my administrative work, and I also use Excel in my role as treasurer for the Local History Society preparing spreadsheets for the accounts.

Liaising with colleagues and other departments and dealing with calls and enquiries to the office has developed my communication skills and telephone manner. I also worked in retail for three years previously, dealing with the public, where I learnt how to answer enquiries and offer help and advice pleasantly and confidently.

I have greatly enjoyed my work at ABC Ltd; however, I also have a keen interest in environmental issues and am an active Member of the Woodland Conservation Volunteer Trust, hence my interest in the job that you are offering.

I would be very happy to discuss my application with you in more detail and look forward to hearing from you in the near future.

Yours sincerely

J. Brown

Jane Brown

EXPERT QUOTE

It's OK to use bullet points in a covering letter to highlight your key competencies; in fact it's a good idea. It often only gets a quick scan to see whether or not the CV is worth reading.

DEBBIE MACEKE, RESOURCE CENTRE MANAGER, ROLLS-ROYCE

EXPERT QUOTE

CVs are strictly factual and practical, but the covering letter is more personal. Reading the covering letter is like looking at the person rather than a piece of paper: you need to get a sense of what someone is offering, what they're bringing to the role, their background and experience.

DAVID GILES, NATALIE WILSHAW AND PAUL TURNER, HUMAN RESOURCES, WESTLAND HELICOPTERS LTD

11
Telephone calls

The phone can be a useful job search tool. Send off a CV or even an e-mail, and you have to wait for a reply. With a phone call, you can find out very quickly if someone is interested or not.

General points

Telephone calls can be:

- information calls;
- speculative calls;
- follow-up calls;
- telephone interviews.

The basic points are the same for all calls. Before picking up the phone make sure:

- You know the name of the person you wish to speak to, unless the call is to find out that information.
- You have the information you need: job advertisement, CV, job description, company information, etc.
- You know what you want to say. Note down the points beforehand.
- You have a diary in case you need to make an appointment.
- You have something to make notes on.
- You won't be disturbed or distracted.

When you are on the phone:

- Smile. It makes your voice sound warmer and more relaxed. You can demonstrate your likeability even on the phone.

- Don't drink, smoke or chew even while the other person is talking. Be professional.

- Make notes – they will come in useful and you can demonstrate your competence and professionalism when they do.

Information calls

Advertisements for vacancies may ask you to phone for further information or an application form. Some companies use the call to screen applicants, and you might be subjected to a short interview to see if you are suitable. Make sure you are prepared before you start. (See the section on page 233 on telephone interviews.)

When calling for information:

- Say why you're calling – 'about the vacancy for...' – and where you saw it.

- Ask for what you want:
  - an application form;
  - a job description;
  - more information;
  - to talk to someone from the department concerned.

- Ask the name of the person to whom you should send the completed application form or CV.

- Take notes of names and extension numbers, and ask for names to be spelled out.

For example, these could be calls to the company reception:

Hello, I'm calling about the vacancy for a Customer Relations Supervisor advertised in this week's *Northampton Advertiser*. Can you put me through to the person dealing with recruitment, please? My name is John Smith.

Hello, my name is John Smith and I'm calling about the vacancy for a Customer Relations Supervisor advertised in this week's *Northampton Advertiser*. Could you send me an application form and a job description, please? My address is 43... Forest Drive... Deansfield... Northampton. The postcode is NO3... 6XY.

Who should I send the form back to? Paula Whitehead; could you spell that please?... And her position is?... Personnel Manager. Thank you.

Hello, could you tell me who's in charge of the Customer Relations Department, please? Mrs Hamblin – could you spell that for me?... And her position is?... Head of Customer Relations, thank you. Could you put me through to Mrs Hamblin, please? My name is John Smith.

Hello, Mrs Hamblin. My name is John Smith. I'm applying for the post of Customer Relations Supervisor and there were one or two points I wanted to clarify. Do you have five minutes to talk?

Good morning, my name is John Smith. I'm applying for the vacancy of Customer Relations Supervisor advertised in this week's *Northampton Advertiser*, and I wanted some more information about the company. Do you have any literature, brochures, an annual report, a company newsletter or magazine?... Thank you, that would be very kind of you. My address is 43... Forest Drive... Deansfield... Northampton. The postcode is NO3... 6XY.

Speculative calls

These calls are similar to speculative letters (see Chapter 14, 'Job search strategies'), and they serve the same purpose: to get you an interview with someone who could give you a job.

When making a speculative call:

- Plan first so you are clear why you are calling and what you can offer.

- Write down the key points you want to cover before making the call.

- Note down names and numbers, and ask for names to be spelled out.

- If the person you want isn't available, avoid leaving a message. Instead, find out when would be a good time to ring back.

- Make sure the person you are speaking to has time to talk. If not, arrange another time to call.

- Explain who you are and why you are calling.

- Be clear about what you can do for the company. Don't leave them to work out how you might fit in.

- Be reasonably persistent, rather than insistent. Be assertive rather than aggressive.

- Suggest options: 'I could call in next week some time. Would Tuesday or Wednesday be convenient for you?'

- If you can't get an interview, try for a consolation prize. These include:
  - an invitation to ring again at a later date;
  - the opportunity to send the organization your CV;
  - contact names in other companies or departments;
  - the name of a recruitment agency the organization regularly uses.

- Whatever the outcome, thank the individual for his or her time.

Here are some examples of more and less successful approaches.

Wait until you're speaking to the right person

Good morning, ABC Finance, how may I help you?

Good morning, I'm calling to see if you have any vacancies for an administrative clerk. I've had a...

No, there are no vacancies that I know of at the moment. I should think anything we did have would be in the Evening Post. *Why don't you have a look in there?*

Find out who to speak to

Good morning, ABC Finance, how may I help you?

Good morning. Could you tell me the name of the person responsible for recruitment, please?

Certainly, that would be Alison Hope in Personnel.

And her position is?

Mrs Hope is the personnel manager.

Thank you. Could you put me through to Mrs Hope? My name is John Smith.

Wait until you can speak to the right person

Good morning, ABC Finance, how may I help you?

Good morning. My name is John Smith. Can you put me through to Mrs Hope in Personnel, please?

I'm sorry, there's no reply from her office. Can I give her a message?

Thank you, but I'd like to speak to her personally. I'll call back later. Can you tell me when it would be a good time to try?

Try after lunch, about one-thirty or two o'clock.

Thank you, I'll call then. Goodbye.

Be gently persistent

Hello, Mrs Hope? My name is John Smith. Do you have five minutes to talk? I'm an experienced administrative clerk with a good understanding of the software packages you use. I'd like to come in to see you to talk to you about any openings you might have.

There are no vacancies here at the moment. Sorry.

I see, but something might become available in the near future. I'd still like to come in and see you, if I may. Would you be free any time in the next week?

How about Monday afternoon, about three-thirty?

That would be fine for me. Where shall I find you?

Ask for me in reception. Oh, and could you bring a copy of your CV with you?

Of course. So that's Monday afternoon, three-thirty, with a copy of my CV. Your main entrance is on Ainsley Road, isn't it? I'll see you Monday, then. Thank you. Goodbye.

If you can't get an interview, try for a consolation prize

No, business is really slack here at the moment. There wouldn't be much point in your coming in.

I see. Could I send you my CV instead, then? You could have a look at my details and if things do pick up, perhaps you would contact me.

Alternatively, ask for contact names in other departments or other companies

No, business is really slack here at the moment. There wouldn't be much point in your coming in.

I see. Do you know of anyone else who might be interested?

Our office suppliers are short-staffed at the moment. I think it might only be temporary, but you could ask them. They're XYZ Supplies, their number is 00000 000000.

Thank you, that's really helpful. Do you have the name of someone there I could contact?

Try Julie Smith. She should be able to tell you who to talk to.

If, despite your efforts, you draw a blank, don't take it personally or let it get you down; just move on to the next call. Every call you make increases your experience and your likelihood of success.

Follow-up calls

Always follow up a speculative CV with a phone call if you want a response.

The general points for follow-up calls are similar to those for speculative calls, bearing in mind that the company should already have a copy of your CV and a covering letter.

- If you said in your covering letter, 'I will call you within the next few days' or 'in the early part of next week', then call within that time.

- Have a copy of your CV and covering letter with you.

- Be prepared to give a brief outline of your CV. The person you speak to might not remember it or have had time to read it.

- If the individual has read it, he or she might want to ask you questions about it.

- Avoid being interviewed over the phone. Ask to see the person instead.

Here are some examples.

Explain why you're calling

Hello, Mr Nichols? I'm John Smith. I sent you a copy of my CV last week along with a letter outlining the ways in which I feel I could contribute to your company. I'm an experienced salesman with a thorough understanding of the agricultural market and an excellent track record. If possible, I'd like to see you to talk about any opportunities you might have coming up in the near future.

The person might not have read your CV

I haven't had time to go through your CV. When was it you sent it?

I understand that you must be very busy. Perhaps I could call in to discuss it with you instead?

There's nothing available here at the moment. Sorry.

I see, but something might become available in the near future. I'd still like to come in and see you, if I may. Would you be free any time in the next week?

OK, as long as you know there's nothing at the moment. How about Monday afternoon, about three-thirty?

That would be fine for me. So that's Monday afternoon at three-thirty, then. Thank you very much. Goodbye.

Be prepared to answer questions

Yes, I did look through your CV. It looks as though it could be of interest. In your position with ABC, you say you were involved with veterinary supplies?

Yes, that's right. I was responsible for introducing the new Vetzyme range. I achieved a target of 43 per cent in the first year in the South West.

However, try to avoid being interviewed on the phone

That sounds OK. How long do you think it would take you to produce a similar result in feedstuffs?

That would be difficult to go into over the phone. Why don't I come and see you? Would you be free any time in the next week?

Telephone interviews

See Chapter 19, 'Interviews and more', for more information about this.

When they call you

While you are looking for a job and could be called by an interested company at any time, *always* check who's calling before you answer so that you can do so professionally and with poise.

If they are calling you, ideally they will first send an e-mail outlining when the call will happen, who will be interviewing you and brief details about what you can expect.

If they call you unexpectedly, stay calm. Remember to make a note of who is calling, from where, and their phone number if it might be different from the one they are calling on.

If possible, get hold of your CV and other useful information. Keep it to hand for just this sort of eventuality. The person calling won't expect you to be as prepared as you would be at a formal interview, but do say more than just yes or no in answer to questions, and make sure you sound enthusiastic and positive and engage with the person calling you.

If you're on a mobile and it's really not an appropriate place to take such an important call, tell them and ask if you can ring them back in a few minutes. Get to the best place you can at short notice – somewhere relatively quiet and calm – before calling back. The same applies if you are in an area with a poor signal.

If you're expecting a call from someone, prepare in advance:

- Check that your voicemail message sounds professional and businesslike. It's also a good idea to ensure it gives your name, if it doesn't already do so, so that the caller knows they have reached the right person.

- Tell any people who might answer your phone – family, flatmates or whoever – what the situation is so that they can be prepared, too.

- If you have given only your mobile number, make sure you keep your phone turned on and charged.

EXPERT QUOTE

Most employers are prepared to have a quick chat with people who call for information, even if it's only to tell them where they advertise vacancies. Make it brief and ask if they have time, first.

MAGGIE FELLOWS, PROJECT MANAGER, SOUTH WEST TUC

12
The job search

You now have all the tools you need to go job hunting. You have a compelling CV, you can write covering letters and make confident phone calls. This chapter and the next two look at how to make effective use of them: how to get your CV in front of people and how to get it working for you, whether it's in an online CV bank, at an agency, or in any of the many methods of job hunting.

Job search stages

It helps to divide your job search into three stages, each of which can be a success or failure in its own right:

- Stage one: Finding enough vacancies to apply for.

- Stage two: Getting interviews.

- Stage three: Getting job offers.

If you are stuck at stage one and not finding enough jobs to apply for, you may find it helpful to read the chapter on 'Job search strategies' and 'Your online job search' to ensure that you are finding all the sources available. If your job is specialized, or if vacancies don't come up very often, see if there are ways you could expand the area in which you are searching: either geographically, looking at different parts of the country or indeed different countries where your skills could be in greater demand or better rewarded, or by broadening your job definition to include related areas of work where your skills could be used.

If you are getting stuck at stage two, applying for plenty of jobs but not getting interviews, you may need to work through previous chapters on writing CVs, application forms and covering letters. It might also be worth reviewing your skills and qualifications: could they be improved and updated in any way?

If you are getting stuck at stage three, getting interviews but not being offered jobs, look at Chapters 15 to 19 on interview skills.

Job market research

Job market research is vital to job hunting. The better informed you are, the more likely you are to pick up on opportunities and openings. The two key things you need are information and contacts.

Getting information

Information helps you build the bigger picture, increases your confidence and helps you to be in the right place at the right time. It could make the difference between finding a job you love, and grabbing what's available. It will help you find out who to contact, how to contact them and what to say, as well as what to put in your CV and letters, and what to include at the interview.

Useful information includes:

- what's happening in your field of work;

- what's changing in that field;

- what's new, what's coming in the future;

- companies who need what you do: who they are, their background, structure, organization and reputation;

- what they do (is it the same as you have always done or are there differences?);

- where they are heading; what's new for them;

- who's moving into the area, geographically or figuratively;

- who's expanding; who's getting new contracts; who's launching new products and so on;

- the key people to contact in these organizations.

All this information is available from a wide variety of sources:

The internet

You can look up company websites, news and chat groups, professional organization and society websites, college and university careers pages, career guidance sites and recruitment agency sites. These will give you detailed information as well as background data, for both your own country and abroad. They might also provide useful links to other sites you may not have considered. Career guidance and recruitment sites might have, or link you to, information about labour market trends, employment profiles, recruitment events and so on. It's worth Googling the name of a company or a job title and seeing what comes up.

Local newspapers, national newspapers and business magazines

These carry features on businesses: who's moving into the area, the local and national economy in general, business reports and profiles, product and service launches, exhibitions and job fairs, open days, local and national promotions, community issues, company relocations and expansions, building and site development, and 'day in the life' features.

Recruitment pages and websites

These can give you a feel for who's hiring and who's firing, who's opening new departments, which jobs are in demand, what sort of skills and experience are being asked for, what sort of salaries are being offered, and which company names crop up again and again.

Trade journals, company newsletters, annual reports and financial reports

Virtually every type of job has its own newspaper or journal that will tell you what is happening. Many of them also include recruitment pages. Company newsletters and annual reports will give you more specific information about companies. You can either see them on the company website or obtain them from the company by writing or phoning.

Trade and business directories will give you information about specific companies, from their name and address to the number of people they employ. There are also directories that will tell you about professional or trade associations, and trade-related journals and publications.

One of the best places to start looking for information is your public library. Here you can get internet access, and find many of the directories, journals and other publications mentioned above. It should also be able to help you find out about professional associations and other organizations that will be useful to you.

What should you do with all this research once you have it? Use it to strengthen your CV, covering letter, and interview preparation:

- Summarize the company's values in two or three points that you can match to your own.

- List three or four things about them that you are enthusiastic about and can mention in your CV, letter and interview.

- List three or four positive points about the company and its place in the market that you can reference in your letter and interview.

- Identify the main problems and opportunities they face in the future and suggest how your skills and experience could make a contribution.

Building contacts

The more people you contact, the more likely you are to find a job. Even if people can't help you directly, they will often put you in touch with someone who can, and they will help you build a more comprehensive picture of what's happening. It's worth spending time building contacts. They are a source of information, help and support that will stand you in good stead for the whole of your life, one way and another. Think creatively about how you can build your network both online and in the real world – you'll need to do both to get the maximum effect.

Networking can be casual, but for your job search you need to be more systematic:

- Research sources of contacts and keep detailed notes.

- Set yourself a target number of people to get in touch with each week or month.

- Keep a record of who you've contacted: names, addresses and helpful information.

- Ask all those you contact if they know anyone else you could speak to.

Even if you feel your current network is thin, there are plenty of sources for contacts.

People

People are a very good source of contacts simply because people know other people. Don't dismiss anyone. Even if someone can't help directly, he or she might know someone who can. Include:

- friends and family, the people who are around you most;

- people you were at school or college with, including lecturers and other staff;

- old colleagues and previous employers;

- business contacts, including suppliers and clients;

- people who contact other businesses through their job, such as solicitors, accountants and anyone who offers business services;

- people you meet at interviews;

- people you meet visiting companies;

- people you meet at trade fairs and open days;

- people you meet on training courses.

Organizations

Organizations and associations are a ready-made network and a way to get to know people you might not meet through social contacts. The sorts of organizations, both online and in the real world, that could be helpful include:

- professional associations;

- trade associations;

- trade unions;

- chartered institutes;

- community organizations;

- special interest groups: women in business, graduate associations, Asian business networks and so on;

- social and leisure groups: health clubs, sports teams, arts groups and so on;

- voluntary organizations and local action groups.

Events

Events are good places to meet people. Make sure you get names and contact details or business cards. You can build good job search contacts at:

- business conferences;

- trade fairs and exhibitions;

- employment fairs;

- company social events;

- professional association events;
- union events;
- training courses, conferences and seminars;
- promotional events;
- open days.

Also contact any company doing the sort of work you want to do. Don't just ask about current vacancies; talk to the staff about:

- the sort of positions and opportunities available in the company;
- what they foresee coming up in the future, both for themselves and for the sector in general;
- the general direction the industry is headed in;
- the company's own development.

Keeping an active network increases your awareness of what opportunities are available; it's like adding extra pairs of eyes and ears. Getting to know people means they get to know you, too. Networking involves telling people about yourself, increasing your visibility and getting your name and face known. It's also about giving as well as taking, and it's a favour you'll be able to repay some day.

Ways of job hunting

There are three approaches you can take to job hunting:

- browsing;
- broadcasting;
- targeting.

Browsing

This is the most widely used job search strategy, and the easiest and least demanding. It involves browsing internet job boards, newspapers and journals looking for advertised vacancies that suit your requirements.

Advantages of browsing

- You have a clear idea of what the advertiser wants and can adapt your CV and covering letter to suit exactly.

- You know there's an actual job available.

- You are contacting companies who are inviting applications.

- You can see the range of what's on offer and can make comparisons between advertisements.

Drawbacks to browsing

- Not all jobs are advertised, or advertised in the places where you are looking.

- You are in competition with everyone else who answers the ad. You'll need to make a strong impression, especially if there's a big response.

- The advertiser has already decided what they want. If they say, for example, that the successful applicant needs a degree, you stand less chance of being interviewed if you haven't got one.

- You are more likely to have to fill in an application form, which could be a drawback if you don't fit neatly into all the boxes.

Browsing will suit you if:

- there are plenty of advertised vacancies in your particular profession or locality;

- you have widely used skills for which there's strong demand;

- you're in a 'high turnover' occupation where vacancies are constantly arising;

- you're confident you can beat the competition.

See Chapter 13, 'Your online job search', for more detailed information about getting the best out of using online job boards.

Broadcasting

This method involves sending your CV by post or e-mail to as many companies as possible in the hope it lands on the right desk at the right time. Another way of doing this is to lodge your CV in a CV bank, where scanning software does the selecting. Broadcasting passively relies on the employer noticing you are a good fit for a job they have got coming up, and asking you along for an interview.

Advantages of broadcasting

- Once you have a CV and covering letter this method needs little extra thought.

- Large numbers of organizations can be contacted in a comparatively short time. You can contact everyone who might be interested in you.

- Getting picked out of a CV bank by scanning software needs little effort on your part.

- Your CV could land on the right desk at the right time and you could get lucky.

Drawbacks to broadcasting

- There is a low response rate – often only one or two replies from a hundred posted or e-mailed CVs.

- You won't know what's happening to your banked CV: who's seen it, whether anybody's seen it, and when, if ever, you can expect a response.

- You may become disillusioned and demoralized because of the poor response.

- Costs can be high if you are sending CVs out by post.

- There is little feedback: you might have only just missed out, but you'll never know.

Broadcasting will suit you if:

- you have standard skills and qualifications that are widely used;

- you have plenty of keywords in your CV for scanning software to pick up;

- you are prepared to work anywhere: CV banks can attract an international response;

- there are lots of companies that can use your particular experience;

- conversely, you need to fish worldwide for the few employers who need your specialized skills, in which case a CV bank is going to be a time- and cost-effective way of advertising yourself to them.

See Chapter 13, 'Your online job search', for more detailed information about getting the best out of CV databanks.

Targeting

This is a selective approach that involves deciding:

- the work you want to do;

- the type of organization you want to work for;

- who, what and where these organizations are;

- who to contact within each one.

Once you have done this, a variety of job search strategies can be used to contact these companies and set up interviews with them. It means taking charge of the search, researching possible employers and selecting suitable targets. This approach is the most active one, taking the most time and energy, but for many people it's also the most effective.

Advantages of targeting

- All your efforts are directed at likely possibilities.

- You get feedback, so you can refine your campaign as you go.

- You can pursue positive responses and let weaker ones pass.

- You can build on your efforts with follow-up calls and letters.

- You are in control of how you present yourself.

- You can adapt your approach to new circumstances that arise.

Drawbacks to targeting

- It needs planning and research to be effective.

- You need to be confident and resilient to approach companies cold and ask if they are interested in you.

- You need persistence and motivation to follow up leads.

Targeting will suit you if:

- you have specific skills and strengths you want to use in your work;

- you wish to get into a particular field of work;

- you have, or are willing to acquire, a thorough knowledge of your particular profession or industry;

- you have a clear career plan;

- you prefer being in control of your search rather than waiting for things to happen.

Using your skills effectively

The key skills that you use in your job search are:

- **job market research**: finding out about companies and organizations, what they want, what they can offer you and what you can offer them;

- **building contacts**: building an effective network;

- **reading advertisements** and job descriptions, analysing their requirements and matching these with your own skills and experience;

- **CV writing**: planning and presenting a CV that showcases your skills and strengths, sells them effectively and gets you interviewed;

- **letter writing**: covering letters and speculative letters that get your CV read with interest;

- **telephone techniques**: getting information and getting your message across;

- **interview skills**: making the right impression face to face.

This book covers all the skills you need for a successful, rewarding job hunt, but there are ways of using your skills effectively so you get the most out of them.

Build on your strengths

Decide what your strengths are and make the best use of them. For example:

- If your strengths lie in building contacts and keeping in touch with people, make good use of networking.

- If your greatest strength is making a good impression and getting on with people face to face, use strategies that bring you into direct contact with employers.

- If you write well, use that strength to craft carefully targeted letters and e-mails to suitable employers.

Manage your weaknesses

Find ways to strengthen, support or overcome any weaknesses that threaten to get in the way of your success:

- **Find out how to do it better, and practise until you improve**. Few people are born knowing how to write a CV, or what to say at an interview. Books like this one show you what you need to know and how to go about it. Once you have the basic skills, practise them until you feel confident. Friends and family can help: ask them to give you a short practice interview or phone call, and give you feedback on how you come across. You can also ask them to look at your CV and covering letters: they can give their reactions and also check for any spelling or grammar mistakes that have slipped through the spellchecker net.

- **Find an alternative**. If you really can't do something, ask yourself if there's a way round it. If you genuinely can't write letters, go to see people. Ring them up and if they ask for your CV, arrange a 10-minute meeting instead. Give them your CV only after you have spoken with them and they have a good impression of you.

- **Find someone else to do it**. The person might either do the job for you (a CV-writing service, for example), or train you to do it and coach you until you improve. Get professional help if you can afford it. If not, swap skills with someone who can do the things you can't, while you help him or her with something he or she is weak on.

- **Make full use of what others have already done**. If your contact-building skills are weak, for example, make use of pre-existing networks such as professional associations, or use an agency that already has the contacts.

EXPERT QUOTE

Adapt your approach to the organization you're dealing with – small companies can be much more flexible than big ones.

DEPARTMENT HEAD, PUBLIC SECTOR

EXPERT QUOTE

I've just taken on someone who went to the effort of finding out who I was and what I did and e-mailed her CV to me. I was impressed with her initiative.

PRODUCER, FILM COMPANY

EXPERT QUOTE

Don't just read the recruitment pages of the newspaper, look in the 'hidden job pages' as well – the business pages.

MARK COLTON, BUSINESS DEVELOPMENT TEAM, JOBCENTREPLUS

13
Your online job search

When you're searching for a job, the internet is probably going to be one of your most useful tools. Like all tools, however, it has its advantages and its drawbacks so this chapter takes a closer look at how you can get the best use out of the internet and how it can help you get ahead of the competition.

What the internet can do for you

Job hunting on the internet is becoming increasingly popular due to the vast amount of online resources available. Throughout this book you will find advice such as visiting employers' websites to gather useful information, or finding professional groups online to network with. But searching specifically for jobs online can take up valuable time that could be used better on other activities. There are thousands of websites to search through, and just typing 'sales manager' or 'accountant' into a search engine will open up an overwhelming number of possibilities, only a small handful of which will actually be relevant to you. One of the key skills you need is the ability to keep this flood of information focused and manageable, while not letting valuable leads get away unnoticed.

Online recruitment resources

There are a number of resources that can make your job search easier, more efficient and more effective.

Job boards

These websites specialize in advertising job vacancies placed by employers and recruitment agencies. They range from big, multi-sector job boards which have vacancies in all industries, to smaller, specialist job sites dedicated to a particular profession or specialization. Most sites are easy to navigate, allowing you to use key words and phrases to narrow your search, and when you find a job that appeals to you, the site will give you full instructions about how to apply online.

When searching for a new job, don't restrict yourself to just one or two sites – use as many job boards as are appropriate to your circumstances. Do your research and find out which sites are relevant to what you are looking for. You can also make full use of any additional services they offer such as job alerts – e-mails that automatically notify you when someone posts a vacancy you might be interested in.

Many job boards also have a facility for posting your CV on their CV databank.

CV databanks

Many job boards and job search sites offer the option of posting your CV on their online database so it's visible to an enormous number of registered recruitment agencies and employers. This service is invaluable; databases are searched by thousands of recruiters – not just every day, but every hour. An increasing number of employers search these databases, so adding your CV to an online database could allow you to be picked for a vacancy you would otherwise never have known existed.

Registration is usually free and you can keep your CV current by updating your profile at any time. Once registered, your CV can be working for you 24 hours a day while you get on with targeted approaches to other employers. If you are concerned about your CV being noticed online by your current employer, make sure the database you choose has a suitable level of privacy control.

Check suitable job boards and databases to see what they can offer you in addition to the basics. Use every tool that could be of service to you. Many job sites offer the opportunity to:

- keep a record of your applications to help you keep track;
- set up e-mail alerts for new vacancies that match your profile;
- upload your CV into a databank, making it automatically available to employers and recruitment agencies;
- store CVs and covering letters online to save time when applying for jobs;
- get tips and advice on everything from CVs to interview techniques;
- use and adapt templates for CVs and covering letters;

- join forums and newsgroups for sharing information and experiences;
- check things like job salary ranges and company profiles to help you make informed decisions.

Other sites will additionally offer, for a fee, more specialist services such as:

- a CV writing service, career coaching and online training;
- access to expert advice on relevant topics via e-mail;
- interactive interview practice via video;
- personality profiling and career assessment;
- job feeds throughout the day, ensuring you hear about new vacancies as soon as they arrive.

Job search engines

These offer a quick and easy way of finding specific job vacancies online. As their name suggests, they are search engines that browse the big job boards, employers' websites, and recruitment agencies' sites, letting you, in effect, explore all these sites in a single search, rather than visiting all the websites individually. When you find something suitable, it will link you directly to the appropriate site.

Recruitment agency websites

Many recruitment agencies now post clients' vacancies directly on their websites. Be a little wary, though. Some of the more unscrupulous agencies have been known to post non-existent vacancies just in order to build up their database of job hunters. It could get very dispiriting if you keep submitting your details and getting no response. If in doubt, phone to find out more about specific vacancies before sending your CV.

Employers' websites

Most companies use their website for recruitment and regularly post job vacancies there. Applying directly through the company site gives you a head start, not only because the vacancy may never appear anywhere else, but because it demonstrates your interest in the organization because you were looking them up.

To find any of the above, just put job board, CV database, job search engine, recruitment agencies, or company or industry name into your main search engine, tailoring as much or as little as you require: 'job board hospitality & catering London', for example, or 'recruitment agencies accounting & finance UK'. Job sites and databanks are usually free to use – the site is paid by the vacancy advertiser – but you may have to pay a fee for some of the more advanced services such as interview coaching or career assessment.

Your online CV

To get your CV noticed on a database, you need to understand how the database works and how recruiters use it. Basically, CVs are screened and selected using keyword scanning – much the same way as you use keywords to find appropriate sites during your own online browsing. Make your CV easy to find:

- **Include keywords**. The scanner can't find what isn't there, so make sure you include those important, specific keywords the scanner is searching for.
  These are:
  - **Occupational background**: career areas such as teaching, engineering, public relations, retailing, financial management, or quality control.
  - **Positions**: actual job titles such as manager, programmer, editor or engineer.
  - **Knowledge areas**: capacity planning, interactive technology, project planning, global markets, product development, restructuring, or systems configuration are examples of the sort of thing you might have knowledge and experience of.
  - **Specific skills and qualifications**: Microsoft Office, BSc in..., MA in..., previous NHS experience, IT (EMIS) competent, Economics graduate, ACA/ACCA qualified, for example.
  - **Workplace skills**: designed, evaluated, organized, represented, developed, analysed, communicated, etc.

  This is yet another reason to study job advertisements and job descriptions intensively before compiling your CV. Extract the keywords and use them as a starting point.

- **Be specific**. If the job description asks for IT proficiency, use the phrase 'IT proficiency' or 'IT proficient' and add your specific skills – Word, Outlook Express, Excel, etc.

- **Go into detail**. Don't just say, for example, you're an IT professional with a range of skills and experience; be explicit:

- four years' experience in IT development;
- experience in Unix Operating System Administration;
- worked as ORACLE DBA;
- wrote reports using Report Writer 2x;
- worked as part of a project team.

Example

Keywords are in bold followed by an explanation in italics:

Career History

2010 to Present ABC **Telecommunications** (*occupational background*)

Customer Services Manager (*position*)

Supervised (*workplace skill*) divisional **customer service** (*occupational background*) department

Organized (*workplace skill*) **staff schedules** (*knowledge area*)

Trained (*workplace skill*) staff in **customer care** (*knowledge area*)

Implemented (*workplace skill*) new **policy procedures** (*knowledge area*)

Monitored (*workplace skill*) service to ensure **targets and objectives** (*knowledge area*) met

Used **Windows XP** (*specific skill*) with **Access** (*specific skill*) for **customer database** (*knowledge area*)

Anticipate variations

Use standard job titles and/or those used in relevant job vacancy adverts. If the most widely used title for your type of job is Media Sales Executive, for example, that's what the scanner will be looking for, not a Media Client Services Manager. If in doubt, include alternative job titles in brackets along with any common abbreviations such as CEO for Chief Executive Officer, for example. Apply the same thinking to your qualifications and skills.

Use the CV registration form

When you put a CV onto a database, you are usually asked to complete a short registration form asking for basic details including your current job title, preferred job target and brief information about the sort of work you're looking for. This information remains, in effect, 'tagged' to your CV, so scanners will pick up data included on this, too. This gives you yet another opportunity to flag up those vitally important keywords and get your CV in front of potential employers.

Keep your CV updated

It's not unusual for recruiters to limit their search to recently submitted CVs. Make sure you keep your CV fresh by resubmitting it regularly – say every six to eight weeks. Take the opportunity to check, update and refresh it at the same time, however minimal the changes – keep your CV live and active.

Maintain a professional appearance

Whether you are e-mailing your CV directly to an employer or uploading it onto an online CV databank, follow exactly the same rules as you would any CV:

- Keep it short and concise.

- Keep it simple so the important information stands out clearly.

- Keep it relevant.

- Make it easy to read.

However, there are some points for directly e-mailed CVs:

- If you're sending your CV as an attached file, include your own name as part of the file name – marysmithcv.doc, for example. It will make it easier to find out of the hundreds of files called cv.doc.

- Even if you are sending your CV to more than one person or applying for more than one job with the same CV, make sure you send each one as a separate, fresh e-mail. Never, ever cc your CV to several different companies at the same time.

- Fill in the subject line. Put the job title and any reference number. Resist the temptation to put anything quirky or hard sell in the hope of getting noticed.

- Check spelling and grammar thoroughly before you click on the send button.

- Get a professional-looking e-mail address – partyanimal@anyisp.co.uk might not be taken seriously.

- Even though it's e-mail, this is a formal job application, so:

    - No abbreviations, jargon or slang.

    - No smiley faces or anything like that.

    - Start and end formally: Dear Ms Smith... Yours sincerely.

    - The contents follow the same rules as covering letters – see Chapter 10, 'Covering letters'.

- Usually you can send your CV as an attachment. If the organization won't accept attached files because of viruses, however, cut and paste your CV into your e-mail and adapt it so it is still attractive and easy to read.

- Don't send large files that will take ages to download. Your CV and covering letter should be okay, but avoid sending large files such as high-resolution photographs or graphics when contacting an employer online. If they are an important part of your job application, as might be in the case of a graphics portfolio, either send a link to your website, or at least alert them and ask permission before sending.

- There are only 25 to 30 lines on that opening e-mail page (depending on the type of font you use) rather than the 50 or so on a sheet of A4 paper, so there is less opportunity to get key points in. But if you don't fit them onto the first screen, the recipient may not bother to scroll down further. Even worse, your CV could be viewed on just a phone screen – you have to give them a really good reason to read on.

- Your name will appear on your e-mail anyway so leave your contact details to the end of your CV. Use the opening screen for important information.

- Arrange that information in a screen-sized chunk that's easy to read and digest at a glance.

- View your CV in the Draft to make sure how you see it is the way it will appear to the recipient. Do the key points stand out? You can format email to some extent, add bullet points, etc, but the simpler you keep it, the more robust it will be.

- Consider carefully options such as adding photographs and signatures. Use your judgement as to whether the result appears more or less professional. Used wisely they can work well, used badly and it could mean your actual information never gets read.

- Your e-mail will include an automatic reply to that address of course, but other e-mail addresses, websites and social media sites should appear as clickable links, too.

The following example shows the career changer's CV on pages 64–65, adapted for e-mail.

Example e-mail CV

Counsellor and Mentor Application

Dear Mr Taylor

Please accept my application for the post of Counsellor and Mentor for North Somerton Young People's Unit. My CV follows.

Personal profile

A fully qualified counsellor with direct experience of supporting young people alongside social services and a background in the voluntary sector. Now seeking the opportunity to develop existing skills, qualifications and experience of working with people in a challenging, stimulating and worthwhile environment.

Key skills

Certificate of Counselling Practice (AEB)

Certificate of Counselling Theory (AEB)

Counselling young people with a variety of problems

Working alongside Social Services

Managing a heavy caseload

Crisis intervention

Dealing with a wide range of people

Career history

VOLUNTEER COUNSELLOR 2012–present: EFG Project

Counselled young people with a range of problems centring on homelessness

Worked on telephone helpline and conducted one-to-one sessions

Worked with Social Services implementing general policy as well as working on specific cases

Gave advice and information about housing and benefit entitlements

Participated in supervision and support meetings

Planned and prioritized a full caseload including crisis intervention when necessary

---

This is roughly the extent of the opening screen.

PATIENT SERVICES TRANSPORT DRIVER 2009–present: XYZ Transport Ltd

Provided driver support for local ring-and-ride health trust scheme

Covered two district outpatients departments, three clinics and three day centres

Collected service users from home, assisted them on and off vehicle and ensured their comfort and safety at all times

Assisted and supported special needs patients as necessary.

cont

DELIVERY DRIVER 2004–2009: Variable

Delivered products to local businesses, maintained full delivery records, schedules and logs.

Education and training

2009–present: XYZ College

Certificate of Counselling Practice (AEB)

Certificate of Counselling Theory (AEB)

1998–2004: ABC School

GCSEs: Seven, including Maths, English and IT.

Personal details

Date of Birth: 15 August 1987

Interests: IT, reading, swimming

Driving Licences: Full, clean UK driving licence, PSV licence.

Contact details

John Smith

1 Anystreet

Anytown AA0 0AA

Tel: 00000 000000

Mobile: 00000 000000

E-mail: jsmith@anyisp.co.uk

Note that this is a very short introduction rather than a full covering letter – the CV does the job instead – and that the personal profile also includes a brief reason why John Smith is applying for the job, which would normally be in the covering letter. There is enough top-quality information in the personal profile and key skills sections to whet the recipient's appetite and tempt them to read on even if it's only these sections that appear on a tiny mobile phone screen.

If you are attaching your CV rather than putting it in the body of the e-mail, make sure you write a full covering letter containing your key strengths, suitability for the job and your reason for applying.

Paper CVs and scanners

Large organizations who receive many applications often use keyword search software to screen all CVs – even paper-based ones sent to them through the post. If this could affect you, make sure your CV is easily read by both an optical scanner and scanning software.

When you are mailing your CV:

- Use plain white paper, printed on one side only.

- Use a clear standard 11- or 12-point font.

- Don't staple or paperclip pages together: the second page might not get read.

- Put your name at the top of each page: detached pages can get misplaced.

- Send it unfolded in an A4 envelope: older scanners sometimes try to read fold lines.

- Go easy on bullet points, italics, etc. Revise your CV so it's as plain as possible while still being readable.

- It's still vitally important to include the keywords the scanner is searching for.

Online extras

As well as using the sites mentioned in this chapter, you can use the internet in other ways to give your job search the edge.

Check your online presence

At the last count, 53 per cent of employers checked applicants' social media presence, and that figure is only going to go up. So maintaining a positive online identity is becoming increasingly important. Put your own name into a search engine and see what comes up, because that's exactly what prospective employers will do when you are being seriously considered for a job.

If you're invisible, you might consider getting a better online presence – joining professional and social networking sites, for example (see below). On the other hand, if what comes up makes you shudder, you might need to do some damage limitation – start actively building a positive presence to redress the balance, and make sure in future that stuff you don't want people to see doesn't get online. Either way, at least forewarned is forearmed.

Build a professional online reputation

Build in professional links wherever possible. Put a LinkedIn link in your CV and covering letter and make sure that you have a complete, up-to-date profile – you have to do more than just register!

Include keywords, just as you would on your CV, and get some activity going – ask questions, join groups and discussions, get recommendations.

Make full use of any profile pages on professional association sites, trade/professional review sites, etc. Contribute to relevant reviews, studies, reports, forums, industry-related blogs and so on, but make sure that everything you do is professional, high standard, and factually correct.

Don't forget that employers could also be checking your Facebook and Twitter presence as well. What are they looking for? Evidence of engagement – community involvement, social breadth, involvement with projects, social initiative. What they least want to find is any evidence of extremism, intolerance or persistent negative attitude. Those are the absolute career killers.

Network

The emergence of professional networking sites – such as LinkedIn, for example – has made networking much easier. So much so that some job sites have direct links to social networking pages. These sites are used by millions of professionals and, used effectively, they can provide a powerful tool in your job search arsenal. Basic accounts are often free and allow you to connect with other people in your profession, along with the people *they* know and so on. There are usually groups covering your particular job or area of interest where you can join discussions and pick up market intelligence. Along with getting news about companies and the state of the job market, you can catch up with colleagues and let the relevant people know you are looking for work. Be aware, though, that an online social networking site is a public space. Nothing is private once it is posted unless you deliberately put a filter on it.

Build your own site

With the facilities around these days, it's perfectly possible to design an easily navigable website or online portfolio for yourself with little or no technical skill. Your own personal site specifically profiling your professional self will give you somewhere where prospective employers can view your work, read your CV and other relevant information, and obtain your contact details. Put 'free build your own website' into a search engine and see what comes up. Select one that best reflects your personality and which will maintain your professional appearance.

Privacy and safety online

It's important to use common sense and caution when you are on the internet. You are giving complete strangers confidential information that, in the wrong hands, could lead to difficult situations and even be quite damaging. Unfortunately, there are programs that crawl the internet seeking out personal information and e-mail addresses and by posting your CV, you become vulnerable to them.

- Be careful about giving out personal information such as your social security number and your date of birth as this type of information can be used by identity thieves.

- Use reputable sites and keep a record of which sites you register with. If you are contacted by a company you don't recognize, ask them to confirm where they got your CV.

- If you're checking a suspicious company, don't just click on the links provided in any e-mails they have sent you; go to their website from an independent, outside source.

- Be suspicious of any offer that seems too good to be true, such as a highly paid job that requires little or no experience. It's possibly a scam, so double-check before submitting any further information. Try putting the company name and 'scam' into a search engine to see if anything comes up. You might not be the first or the only person they've contacted.

- No legitimate job agency ever requires payment up front from the applicant.

- Nor do they need your bank details.

- Control unwanted e-mail – spam – by setting up a separate, dedicated e-mail address for your job search.

- Use a different user name and password from your private and work ones for job search and career networking sites.

EXPERT QUOTE

We use online applications. At the moment, we screen them personally but the next step will be to use software. When that happens, the keywords will all be in the advertisement and if they aren't included your application won't be selected.

DEBBIE MACEKE, RESOURCE CENTRE MANAGER, ROLLS-ROYCE

14
Job search strategies

There are at least nine different methods of job hunting. The aim of all of them is to put you in contact with potential employers with a view to getting an interview. The best strategies to use are those suited to your own personality and the type of job you want, but the more you try, the greater your chance of success.

The nine strategies are:

- answering advertisements for vacancies;
- CV and follow-up call;
- personal letter;
- recruitment agencies;
- networking;
- job fairs;
- personal appearances;
- foot in the door;
- unconventional approaches.

Answering advertisements for vacancies

This strategy has already been covered in the section on browsing in 'Ways of job hunting' in Chapter 12. Whether you find the advertised job online or in print, plan carefully before responding. There's only one chance to apply, and it needs to be as good as you can make it because you will be in competition with every other applicant.

Answering advertised vacancies will appeal to you if:

- there is a trade journal or website that carries quality job ads that suit your skills and experience;

- plenty of vacancies come up in your type of work;

- you live in or are moving to a particular location and can use the geographical selection feature on recruitment websites along with local papers to find work close to home;

- your career history is straightforward and works well on a standard application form.

Getting the best out of applying for advertised vacancies

- Make sure your CV for each application reflects what is needed in the job – see Chapter 3.

- Customize each covering letter so it addresses the specific requirements of that job for that company. See Chapters 3 and 10.

- When applying online, don't use the standard CV template provided if it doesn't showcase your talents and experience as you would like. Use your own format instead, if the site will let you do that.

- When applying online, assume scanning software will be used to pick out suitable applicants. Use keywords.

- Find good sources of advertisements – internet sites and journals geared to the type of job you want.

- Don't forget your local job centre. It provides a central information point and access to an extensive job bank for your local area, the UK and European Union.

See the previous chapter for more detailed information about getting the best out of job boards.

CV and follow-up call

Your CV and a covering letter are mailed or e-mailed to companies you have targeted, followed by a call to gauge the result, and where possible arrange a meeting. For this method to be successful your CV must be tailored to the type of employer you are contacting and the sort of employment you are seeking. Your covering letter must be attention-getting and your follow-up call confident and positive.

Find out who's interested in what you are offering with a preliminary phone call to establish whether people would like to see your CV. Avoid an on-the-spot telephone interview, though.

This method will appeal to you if you:

- know the market and the companies likely to be interested in your skills;

- have a good CV that sells your skills and accomplishments;

- are confident about putting your skills across, both in writing and on the phone.

Getting the best out of a CV and follow-up call

- Always e-mail or write to a named individual. Find out his or her job title, too. A CV and call to a named person stand more chance of getting a response. Ones sent to 'Dear Sir or Madam' or 'Dear Head of Human Resources' often end up in the bin.

- Do as much research and targeting as possible before you contact anyone.

- Don't be afraid to phone and ask for information.

- You don't have a job advertisement to tell you what the organization wants, so you need to understand what its needs are likely to be. This is where networking and research help, along with your own personal knowledge and experience.

- Use your covering letter to introduce yourself, your skills, your interest in the company, and your knowledge and understanding of the job. Present yourself as a potentially useful member of the team.

- Always follow up when you say you will. Have a copy of your CV and covering letter handy when you phone.

- Always follow up. Don't expect the organization to ring you, or think it will if it is interested enough. Someone might, but then again he or she might forget, or lose your number, or mean to do it next week, when he or she has cleared their in-tray or got back from holiday.

Personal letter

This is similar to the method above, but the emphasis is on the letter. E-mail or write to a key person about a relevant topic you have heard of through your network or the media: news of expansion or relocation, or a new contract or product, for example. Say how you can be of help to the company in this situation, and outline your relevant skills and experience that could be particularly valuable to it.

Each letter must be personal, topical and accurately targeted to achieve its objective: a meeting to discuss things further. Your CV should support what you say in the letter. Follow up with a personal call.

This method will appeal to you if you:

- have, or can achieve, a sound knowledge of what's going on in your field;

- keep in touch with the news in your profession or locality;

- write clearly and persuasively;

- are confident about your skills and your ability to contribute;

- are willing to build a longer-term relationship with an organization without necessarily getting an immediate pay-off.

Getting the best out of personal letters

- All the points outlined for a CV and follow-up call apply here, too.

- Be the solution to a problem. What knowledge and experience do you have that the organization could use just now?

- Use your covering letter to demonstrate you understand the organization's current needs and how valuable your knowledge or experience would be to it.

Recruitment agencies

These can be very helpful, particularly if there are specialist agencies for your type of work: engineering, secretarial or IT, for example. Agencies have all the advantages of knowing the job market well:

- They know what's happening currently and can make informed guesses about the future.

- They know where the jobs are.

- They know who to contact.

- If you choose the right one, it will have an established reputation with suitable employers.

Visit agency websites to register and see what they have available, but try to meet them face to face as well, where possible. Treat an interview with an agency, however informal, as you would one with an employer. They are assessing your suitability for various positions and will be selling you on the strength of what they see. Dress and behave accordingly. Keep in regular contact, but be careful not to pester the agency unnecessarily.

Agencies will appeal to you if you:

- have marketable skills;

- have experience in your chosen field;

- are prepared to keep in regular contact.

Getting the best out of recruitment agencies

- Use e-mail, phone and face-to-face meetings to build a relationship with the agency staff. Where possible, stick with an individual consultant who can get to know you and your strengths and requirements.

- Be clear about what you want and don't want from the start. Be open-minded, but if the agency repeatedly puts you up for jobs that aren't suitable, find out why.

- Be selective about which agencies you register with. Talk to each agency before making a commitment, and sign up with two or three of the most suitable. Spread your options and increase your chance of success, but resist registering with every single one on the off chance that they will come up with something.

- Be honest with the agency and give them as much information as they need. If some of it is sensitive or confidential, make sure the consultant knows this.

- Most recruitment consultants are experienced and know the current job market. Respect their advice and take advantage of any help they can give you with your CV or interview skills.

- Keep in touch regularly. About once a week shows commitment without harassment. Make sure you know:
  - who the agency is sending your CV to;
  - any feedback it's getting, positive and negative;
  - full details about any job you are actually being interviewed for;
  - any information about the company or job that would be useful to you.

Networking

This method supports many of the other methods, and uses your professional and social contacts to help you get in touch with employers who might not otherwise be accessible. People and organizations in your network can help by:

- giving you information;
- allowing their name to be used as an introduction;
- introducing you personally;
- speaking to others on your behalf;
- recommending you either in person or in writing.

Networking will appeal to you if you:

- have a wide range of contacts;
- have access to ready-made networks such as professional and trade associations either online or in the real world;
- have the interpersonal and social skills to access help;
- are good at following up leads and introductions;
- are happy to build long-term relationships, rather than looking for an immediate pay-off.

Getting the best out of networking

- Thank people for any help, advice, leads or introductions they have given you, and return the favour when you can.

- Get in touch with existing contacts. Let people know you are looking for a job and would be grateful for any leads they can give you. Call or e-mail everyone you know. Even the most unlikely person could turn out to know somebody you need to talk to.

- Build up new contacts. Actively search out opportunities, online or in the real world, to meet and talk with people who will expand your contact list.

- Always get contact details or business cards from contacts and file them safely, even if you are absolutely certain you will remember them. Add the companies they work for, job titles, and a brief note of how they have helped you and what action you have taken, or intend to take.

- Follow up every lead, however unlikely. If you don't take advice, people will eventually stop giving it. When you get a positive result, let your informant know about it.

Job fairs

Job fairs are excellent networking occasions, the opportunity to meet a number of potential employers. They offer a chance to see and be seen, as well as get a broad picture of what's happening. There are two sorts: career fairs, which are a chance to meet and talk to company representatives, and actual recruitment fairs, where the companies that attend have vacancies that need filling.

Job fairs will appeal to you if:

- there are regular job fairs that cover your areas of interest;
- you present yourself well and have good interpersonal skills; you can talk to people easily and ask relevant questions;
- you are organized enough to make notes, keep and file brochures and business cards, and follow up contacts.

Getting the best out of job fairs

Whether it's a career fair or a recruitment fair:

- Take copies of your CV – 20 or 30, depending on the size of the fair, unfolded, unstapled and in a folder to keep them clean and uncreased.
- Find out who will be there and do some research before you go. Talking intelligently about a company to its representative and asking interesting questions will make you stand out.
- A job fair is a formal occasion; dress and behave as you would for an interview.
- Get the names and job titles of people you talk to. Follow up with a letter saying how much you appreciated the conversation, how interested you are in the company, and recapping your particular skills and strengths.

Personal appearances

This means visiting the place where you want to work, either on spec or following a phone call. The aim is to see the person who could hire you and set up an interview, either then and there or at a later date. This method is particularly useful where personal qualities are important – a friendly and persuasive manner, for example – which might not come across in a CV or letter. It's also effective when actual skills need to be demonstrated or shown – an artist or designer showing a portfolio, for instance.

The approach must be made confidently and positively. It helps to know as much as possible about the company beforehand, and it will certainly increase your self-confidence. It's also useful to know the name of the person you want to see. An approach to a named individual stands more chance of a response than a general enquiry, so use network contacts and/or website information to find out who the most relevant person would be.

Making a personal appearance will appeal to you if you:

- have good presentation and interpersonal skills;

- have a relevant personal quality that doesn't come across in a CV;

- need to demonstrate your skill in person.

Getting the best out of personal appearances

- Dress appropriately. Treat the meeting as you would any formal interview.

- Take your CV, but only leave it with the contact after he or she has seen you and formed a good impression. Make sure it backs up everything you say at the meeting.

- Take any relevant material. Practise making a short presentation until you can do it confidently.

- Do your research before you go. Being well informed is essential to making a good impression. Plan what questions you want to ask beforehand.

- Give a succinct, two-minute or less outline of your background, highlighting your experience and your particular skills and strengths – a 'verbal CV'. Finish off with the reason you are interested in a job with this particular company and what you believe you can offer it. Plan it beforehand and practise until you are fluent.

- If the organization doesn't have a suitable job, use the meeting as a networking opportunity. Ask if your contact knows of anyone else who might be interested in what you have to offer. Ask if you can use his or her name as an introduction when you contact this new company.

- Follow up with a letter or e-mail thanking the person for his or her time, saying how interested you are in the company and reviewing your skills and strengths.

Foot in the door

This means getting inside a company, whether for an informal interview or a six-month internship or work placement.

While the disadvantages of this method are clear – it's time-consuming and you won't necessarily get paid – the advantages can outweigh them. It's a chance to:

- build up contacts and networks;
- see what goes on day to day in that environment;
- let others see what you can do;
- familiarize yourself with new technology or practices;
- get a feel for that type of work or organization;
- raise your profile with that employer or in that line of work;
- build up your experience and track record.

Ways of achieving a foot in the door include:

- informal or information interviews;
- open days;
- short contract or project work;
- work placement;
- internships;
- temporary working;
- part-time work;
- voluntary work.

A foot-in-the-door approach will appeal to you if you:

- are confident of your ability to perform your chosen job well;
- are interested and enthusiastic about your work;
- need the specific experience more than you need the pay;
- are radically changing what you do, or have just come out of education, and need more knowledge to base future decisions on;

- are radically changing what you do, or have just come out of education, and need concrete experience to put in your CV.

Getting the best out of foot in the door

- Network, network, network. Meet and talk to anyone you can: colleagues, clients, suppliers, everyone.

- Keep your eyes and ears open and ask intelligent questions at every opportunity.

- Volunteer for anything that means extra experience, responsibilities or duties, or that gets you to meet people.

- Keep in mind the three key things you are looking for:
  - the offer of a permanent job;
  - experience and skills to go on your CV;
  - networking contacts.

Unconventional approaches

These are unusual methods that have worked for some people. They are based on the marketing and PR methods used by small businesses to increase custom, and are often best suited to more creative or publicity-oriented fields of employment, where they can work very well.

Possibilities include:

- Direct mail: promotional material such as high-quality graphics, brochures or leaflets, sent or e-mailed to suitable targets in place of an ordinary CV.

- Raising your public profile. Demonstrate your expertise by volunteering to speak at conferences, workshops and seminars.

- Getting into print. Trade and professional journals are often interested in articles from people in their specialist area.

- Developing a blog. Establish your knowledge and insight and enhance your profile with a positive, upbeat or even humorous internet presence.

- Self-advertisement – in newspapers or journals, or on your own website. The local and trade press are often on the lookout for something unusual or entertaining.

- An offer people can't refuse: to work for nothing, to double profits, anything that means laying your cards on the table and taking a gamble.

It is essential that anything you do is well researched and targeted and executed competently. Methods like these raise your profile and help to open doors, but you will still need conventional job search methods to approach potential employers rather than hoping that they will contact you.

This will appeal to you if you:

- are in a creative or publicity-oriented field;

- are very confident of your ability;

- have the presentation skills for the method you have chosen;

- know your market well enough to predict the outcome;

- are certain your reputation will be enhanced;

- are actively supporting your job with other approaches.

Getting the best out of unconventional approaches

- Research thoroughly before you start. Know what message you need to get across and how that can be done effectively in the market you have chosen.

- Go for quality rather than quantity. Always aim for the highest standard if you want to make a good impression.

- Strike while the iron's hot. Contact prospective employers while your name is in print, your article is current or you are on the speakers' programme for the next conference.

- Use anything you do as a networking opportunity. Send copies of articles to interested contacts; send them invitations to seminars and so on. The aim is to raise your profile and get people talking about you in a positive way.

EXPERT QUOTE

When we moved into our new offices, one of the first letters we got was a CV from someone who lived nearby. She did temporary cover for us and now has a permanent job.

MANAGING DIRECTOR, BUSINESS SUPPLY COMPANY

EXPERT QUOTE

Find out who's responsible for recruitment and talk to them. It's not necessarily anyone in personnel, it can be the shop-floor manager, for example. Ring up and find out.

MARK COLTON, BUSINESS DEVELOPMENT TEAM, JOBCENTREPLUS

EXPERT QUOTE

We aim to reply to all speculative CVs. If they're suitable, we keep them on a database for 6 to 12 months and contact them if a job becomes available in that time.

DEBBIE MACEKE, RESOURCE CENTRE MANAGER, ROLLS-ROYCE

EXPERT QUOTE

Advertising costs money. I acknowledge all CVs that I get sent and say if they're of interest or not. I keep suitable ones on file for six months or so and when a vacancy comes up I look through these first. Why would I spend hundreds of pounds on advertising when the right person is often already on file?

DIRECTOR, MANUFACTURING COMPANY

EXPERT QUOTE

Make sure you send your CV to the right person. My name is on the website, so I don't appreciate being called 'sir or madam'. There's no excuse for careless mistakes, either. We get letters that are obviously broadcast copies sent to dozens of companies with just the name changed. Being told that someone 'always wanted to work for British Aerospace' does give it away a bit.

DAVID GILES, NATALIE WILSHAW AND PAUL TURNER, HUMAN RESOURCES, WESTLAND HELICOPTERS LTD

15
Interviews: making a great impression

Congratulations. Your CV has done its job and they want to see you for an interview. What do you do now? This section looks at all aspects of the interview, from making a great first impression to what to say when the panel ask if you have any questions for them. It also looks at different types of interview, from panel interviews to assessment centres, and at what else can happen at interviews: aptitude tests and psychometric tests, for example.

Why have an interview?

Why can't employers decide from your CV whether you can do the job or not? Why do they need to see you? If they are interviewing you, you can be sure you are one of the dozen or so applicants who have:

- the essential skills, qualifications, abilities and achievements;

- the desirable skills, qualifications, abilities and achievements they would like;

- suitable knowledge and experience;

- an appropriate career development path;

- sufficient consistency and stability of employment to make you a dependable employee.

Your potential employer now needs to make sure you are:

- Someone who *can* do the job. That is, someone who has:
  - the knowledge;
  - the skills;
  - the experience.
- Someone who *will* do the job. You must be someone who has:
  - the personal characteristics;
  - the enthusiasm and commitment necessary.

The point of the interview is to investigate those key areas more thoroughly. The employer will need to:

- **check** you have the relevant skills and experience stated in your CV;
- **clarify** any puzzling, missing or unfavourable information;
- **complete** the picture of you presented by your CV.

What happens at an interview

Most interviewers try to make the structure of the interview the same for each candidate and they usually follow a basic outline.

The welcome

Designed to put you at your ease, this usually includes introductions and a brief, ice-breaking chat. This is usually followed by a brief account of the job and the company, and an outline of what will happen in the rest of the interview.

Structured questions

Interviewers then go on to ask questions designed to probe your skills and experience. They often have a list of standard questions they ask every applicant, based on the requirements detailed in the job description. They will sometimes start this part of the interview by asking you to give a run-down of your current post, or to describe your responsibilities. The aim of open questions like these is to see how you use your knowledge, skills and abilities in your present job.

Person-specific questions

The interviewer then goes on to ask questions specifically related to what you have put on your CV. This is sometimes thought of as the tricky part of the interview, where employers probe into any weaknesses they might have spotted. Looked at positively, however, it's your chance to come across as an individual with a unique career history, and to reassure them about any reservations they may have.

Questions usually follow a logical structure and an orderly sequence. Towards the end of the interview, however, the interviewer might decide he or she needs more information about something covered earlier, so don't be unsettled if the interviewer goes back to a previous question. Just give as much information as you can.

Your questions for the interviewer

When they have all the information they want, interviewers will ask if you have any questions for them. Always have something ready. Good, intelligent questions at this stage make an impression, and this is covered in a future chapter.

The finish

Interviewers will usually tell you what's going to happen next: whether there are any further stages such as a second interview or assessment tests, for example. They should tell you when you can expect to hear the result, and whether they will ring or write with their decision. If they offer travel expenses, this is the time to sort them out. The interview usually ends with the interviewer thanking you for coming.

Preparing for the interview

If you want to have a great interview, make sure that you:

- know from the job ad, the job description, and any other information exactly what the job entails;

- have the skills and competencies required;

- can give examples of how, when and where you have demonstrated these competencies in the past;

- can present these examples confidently and enthusiastically;

- display in your appearance and behaviour the personal qualities the organization wants.

The key to a great interview is preparation. Invest time and effort beforehand to ensure you feel confident and present a positive image on the day.

Interviews differ in detail, but you can be certain that every interviewer will question you thoroughly about the skills, qualifications and personal qualities mentioned in the job ad and the job description. Interviewers will also question you about areas of your CV where they perceive the match is weak. They will expect you to know something about the organization you hope to work for, why you want the job and why you think you would do it well. Your preparation therefore needs to include:

- evidence that you have the skills, qualities and experience they need;
- explanations for the parts of your CV where you are weakest;
- knowledge of the industry or sector in general, and this company in particular;
- good reasons why you are applying for the job.

Evidence of your skills

Interviewers can't come and watch you doing your job, so you need some other way of convincing them you know what to do. You need examples of times you have successfully displayed your skills and qualities, and which demonstrate your areas of experience. Reread the advertisement, the job description and any other information you have. Make sure you know the responsibilities and duties the job entails, and what skills, qualities, experience and qualifications are required. See Chapters 1 and 2.

Work through the information, underlining key points such as:

- specific skills;
- areas of experience;
- responsibilities;
- qualifications and training;
- knowledge areas;
- qualities and characteristics;
- abilities.

List everything, then write down how, when and where you have demonstrated each requirement. If, for example, the ad asks for someone calm under pressure, you might recall a time an order had to be completed ahead of schedule and how you kept calm, organized yourself and prioritized the workload so you could meet the deadline and save the company a large penalty charge. Make sure you have at least one good example for each requirement. If your current job can't supply an example, think of one from:

- previous jobs;

- unpaid positions: voluntary work, community associations, organizations and sports teams;

- your personal life.

Turn these notes into interesting, concise anecdotes. If the interviewer asks, 'How would you cope with an aggressive customer?', rather than saying, 'I would do x, y and z,' tell him or her about an occasion when you dealt tactfully and successfully with a belligerent customer in real life. Commit these examples to memory and practise delivering them until you feel confident. At the interview, nerves could make you forgetful, so rehearse your key answers until they flow easily. If possible, role play with a friend so you get used to doing it beforehand, listening out for opportunities to present your evidence even when the questions are differently phrased.

Explaining gaps

Check your CV against the job description. Are there any obvious gaps such as:

- shortage of relevant skills or experience?

- shortage of experience in certain areas?

- lack of qualifications?

If there are, you will be asked about them. Anticipate and prepare as thoroughly as possible in advance. You may end up being over-prepared, with answers to questions that aren't even asked, but you'll feel far more confident going into the interview knowing that you have well thought-out answers rather than going in dreading any awkward questions.

- Where you have missed out information on skills or experience, perhaps by not knowing they were relevant, supply evidence in the interview – anecdotes and examples – to demonstrate your competence.

- If you lack specific workplace experience, tell the interviewer what you did in similar situations in voluntary work or your outside interests, and how you relate this to your intended job.

- Does your practical experience make up for a lack of qualifications or training? Older, experienced people can get promoted to jobs that demand a degree from a new starter.

- Will training fill the gap? Are you willing to train, possibly in your own time or at your own expense? It would help if you can give examples of how quickly you have picked things up in the past, or how successfully you managed to juggle work and training.

Another problem on your CV could be anything that hints that you have had employment problems in the past, such as:

- gaps in employment;

- frequent job changes;

- moves backwards or sideways;

- abrupt career changes;

- inconsistent choices of work.

As above, prepare in advance. Don't lie, but consider how to present any problems in the best possible way. If you have good reasons for employment gaps or job changes, give them. If you have been travelling, for example, tell the interviewer what you learned during that time that will be relevant to the job: how you got on with people from all walks of life, or coped with challenges, for example. Make it clear that whatever caused the gap is no longer relevant and won't be a problem for the employer.

If you don't have good reasons, explain the circumstances and any contributing factors. Don't sound as if you are making excuses for yourself, but emphasize that you are a very different person now, and describe in what way.

Industry knowledge

We have already looked at how important getting industry knowledge is for preparing your CV and for finding who to apply to. It's just as important when you prepare yourself for the interview. The more senior the position, the more the interviewers will expect you to know, but at any level, company knowledge wins you gold stars at interview. A good grounding in company background helps your confidence and enhances your performance. It also helps you to decide whether you want to work for the particular company, and why.

As well as getting a general outline of the company, you might like to research the following specific questions.

What does the company do?

- What are its products and/or services?
- What is its profile in the marketplace? How does it like to be seen?
- How and where are its goods or services produced?
- How are they provided or distributed?

Who does it do it for?

- What is the market for these goods or services?
- Who are the actual customers?
- Is the market expanding or contracting?
- What is the company doing about it in either case?

How is the company organized?

- How big is the company?
- Is it a single company or a conglomerate?
- Is it a multinational?
- Are there lots of subsidiaries and divisions, or is everything centralized?
- How is the relevant part of it structured?

What's the competition?

- Who are its competitors?
- What are they currently doing?
- How does it position itself against them?

What's its history?

- Where did it come from; when was it established, how did it start out and how was it built up?
- What are its biggest achievements?
- Was it at one time bigger or smaller?
- Is the area you are entering increasing or decreasing in size, prestige, etc?

- Have there been takeovers, mergers, buy-outs, downsizing?
- What has changed radically over the years?

What's its future?

- What is the company's vision? Does it have a mission statement?
- What are the current priorities?
- What are its prospects?
- What are its major current and future projects (as far as you can legitimately find out)?
- What is the biggest threat currently facing the company and/or the industry as a whole?
- What is the greatest opportunity confronting it?

Why you want the job

You need to be clear about how well you fit the job profile, how this job fits your career progression and overall goals, and how it leads on from your current job. Decide what you can bring to the job, rather than what you can get from it, and show that the job:

- matches your skills and abilities;
- develops naturally from your existing experience;
- gives you the chance to use those skills to tackle the company's problems;
- presents you with challenges you have the background and experience to deal with successfully;
- gives you the opportunity to play a key role in an organization or industry you respect.

Making a good impression

First impressions count at interview. How you respond to questions, how you dress and your body language create a picture of you that can't be seen from your CV. Interviewers already know about your skills, qualifications and experience. What they need to see at the interview are your personality and enthusiasm.

Don't feel you need to put on an act and pretend to be something you're not – super-confident, bubbly or a high flier. Be yourself, but be your best self – happy, confident, keen and alert.

As we saw in Chapter 2, what organizations want from their workforce is contribution, cultural fit, motivation and engagement. The personal qualities that deliver this are highly valued and it will help you if you can express them at the interview.

To recap, they are:

- likeability;
- intelligence;
- positivity;
- competence;
- integrity;
- adaptability.

Likeability

Most employers want employees who are open, cooperative and communicative. You know yourself that you feel more comfortable with people who are friendly and open than with those who are reserved and stiff, and interviewers are no different.

Agreeable people are much more pleasant to work with and get on with their colleagues better, so, naturally, employers will be looking for these traits during the interview and by being open and responsive you will achieve a head start. Remember to smile and be forthcoming – don't make the interviewer dig the information out of you. Avoid one-word, 'yes–no' answers if you possibly can, and always give a full reply including relevant anecdotes to illustrate key points.

Intelligence

Demonstrate your intelligence by being curious – ask questions and listen to the replies with interest. Questions can show your grasp of your profession and knowledge of the company, and also demonstrate your enthusiasm for the sort of work you do and the job you're applying for.

Interviewers naturally look more kindly on people who they feel will give 100 per cent than on those who may be better qualified on paper but appear less engaged, so be interested in what the interviewer is saying. Listen, smile and nod when they tell you things and answer with enthusiasm. Genuine interest, sincerely shown, will increase your chances at interview enormously.

Positivity

Sit up straight, look alert, speak clearly, smile and make eye contact so that the interviewer sees someone positive, assured, optimistic and constructive – someone who will tackle problems and who will be positive to work with.

Confidence is a quality you must project. You needn't be pushy, smug or arrogant, but you do need to project a quiet, positive confidence in yourself and your abilities. The employer needs to be able to trust you to do the job and if you sound negative, you undermine that trust.

Always answer positively – don't apologize for what you see as shortcomings:

Example

The interviewer asks, *'This job requires an understanding of spreadsheets. Would you say you had that?'*

You could reply: 'I'm sorry, I've used them to do the household accounts, but that's all, I'm afraid.'

Or you could give a positive response: 'Yes, I would. I use Microsoft Excel to do all the household accounts, so I'm quite used to it. I'm sure I could quickly become familiar with its commercial use.'

However nervous you are, make sure your voice sounds confident:

- Pause and take a full breath before speaking. This relaxes your vocal cords and steadies your voice.
- Speak a little lower than normal, projecting from your diaphragm rather than your throat. This stops your voice sounding shrill and strangled.
- Speak a little slower and more clearly than you normally do. It stops you gabbling and saying things without thinking, and it gives you gravitas.
- Remember to smile; it warms your voice and relaxes your lip and cheek muscles.

You'll need to volunteer positive information about yourself and your abilities. In other words, you need to be able to blow your own trumpet – something not many of us are good at doing. How do you put your points across without sounding as if you're bragging all the time? When you start to feel uncomfortable with 'I am...' and 'I can...', try ringing the changes with:

- 'I would say that I...'

- 'I believe I am...'

- 'My past record suggests...'

- 'My experience tells me...'

- 'People have told me I...'

- 'Colleagues tell me that...'

- 'My boss would probably say...'

- 'Friends say that I...'

Competence

The first thing is to simply turn up at the right place, on time and fully prepared. Present yourself well – well groomed and smart – and make sure you arrive with any material you may need such as a notepad, a copy of your CV, any presentation materials you've been asked to bring, etc.

If you've been sent details of the interview keep them handy. Nerves make you forget things – the name of the person interviewing you, which floor of the building they're on, all sorts of things. It has been known for interviewees to turn up at large multi-occupancy office buildings only to find that, although they memorized the address, they've forgotten the name of the company actually holding the interview.

Integrity

Many interviewers rely on old-fashioned gut instinct to tell them whether someone is honest so demonstrate your trustworthiness in the traditional ways – offer a firm handshake, look the interviewer in the eye, listen attentively and avoid distracting nervous habits. They will often ask questions that directly address this quality so listen out for questions such as:

- In what areas are you weakest?

- What sort of problems do you find hardest to deal with?

- What is the hardest professional hurdle you've ever had to face?

- Describe a time when you had to admit to a mistake.

- Can you describe a time at work when you had to ask for help from your manager?

- Describe a time when you spoke out against general opinion.

- What is your attitude to risk?

- Which sorts of clients do you find you have most problems with?

Each of these questions is designed to evaluate your honesty, integrity and self-awareness. Answer honestly and professionally in a way relevant to the job in question and avoid over-sharing on the one hand or bluff and bluster on the other.

Adaptability

Demonstrate positive energy and enthusiasm to the whole challenge of starting a new job and meeting new people. Show your adaptability by being willing to learn and grow – express an interest in developing your existing skills and knowledge further, and in opportunities for new experiences and responsibilities. If anything unexpected happens during the interview, remain poised and react calmly and confidently. Show that you can adapt readily to the requirements of a changing situation.

Think about how, when and where you have demonstrated these qualities, because it's important that you go to the interview armed with this evidence of your employability. The interviewer already knows you have most of the necessary competencies — that's why they're interviewing you. One of the main reasons they now want to meet you in person is to gauge your personal attributes and attitudes and see whether your skills are underpinned by the sort of qualities that can be of use in the job and which will make you an asset to the organization. You need to demonstrate them just as thoroughly at the interview as you would any of your other workplace skills and experience.

Imagine, for example, a well-qualified candidate who perfectly matches the job description and who goes to the interview fully prepared to talk about his skills and qualifications. He feels he has done well in the interview and is bewildered not to be offered the job. This happens not once but several times.

Eventually he interviews with a company that offers feedback and they tell him that while they had been impressed by his skills and experience, they felt he came across as reserved and unengaged, even a bit superior. He realizes he has been so focused on getting his skills across and being a perfect match, he has come over as being a bit of an automaton – all work and no personality. Employers are worried about his ability to fit in, get on with his colleagues and work as part of a team.

He gives more thought to demonstrating his personal qualities and focuses on his likeability and positivity. At his next interview he relaxes, smiles more and is warmer and more friendly towards the interviewer – much more his natural self. As well as that, he expresses more of an interest in the company and the work of the department, asking relevant questions and bringing more of his knowledge about the company culture and values into his responses. He also emphasizes his role working as part of a team in a couple of his answers, showing how he contributed to their success rather than focusing on his personal performance alone. The result is much more positive and it isn't long before he lands a job.

Looking the part

The interviewer forms an opinion of you the minute you step through the door. Your appearance needs to express the same message that your answers to the interviewer's questions will do – that you are professional, confident and experienced, and can do the job. Everything about you should support this image of professionalism, from the clothes you wear to the way you sit.

Your general appearance

You need to look clean, groomed and smart. Extra attention to detail – clean fingernails and polished shoes – helps to make you feel confident and show you have made an effort, something interviewers like to see.

How you dress

The current work ethic is about teamwork, so dress as if you belong to the organization – a smarter version of the people it already employs. If you are applying for a job you already know well, you will know what the dress code is. If you are entering a new industry, do some research to find out what applies. Look at company brochures and newsletters to see the image they project. Photographs of people in formal suits and ties tell you that a smart suit, for both men and women, is required for the interview. However, if the annual report shows pictures of the staff in jeans and T-shirts, then extra-smart casual wear might fit in better.

If in doubt, ask someone who works in that type of job what he or she recommends, go to see what employees entering and leaving the building are wearing, or simply ring the company, say you have an interview there, and ask what the dress code is.

Whether you are dressed in a three-piece suit or chinos, you need to present a highly professional appearance:

- Be well pressed, clean, fresh and tidy.

- Dress as if going to an important meeting or presentation rather than for your average day.

- Remember that quality shows. Well-cut, well-finished clothes in natural fibres give the right impression, whether a formal suit or business casual wear.

- Dark colours convey authority better than light ones.

- Plain colours are less distracting than busy patterns.

- Avoid:
  - anything too short or too tight;
  - extremes: go for neutral styles, colours, etc;
  - fussy, distracting accessories;
  - novelty ties, earrings, bags or briefcases, which will undermine your professionalism.

- If you buy a new outfit, wear it a couple of times before the interview, even if only at home. Make sure it's comfortable and that you can sit down without anything riding up or twisting round, and that you can stand up and shake hands without anything gaping or straining.

Posture

Project your confidence, capability and interest in the way you carry yourself:

- Stand tall – stomach in, head up, shoulders back.

- Be poised and alert in your manner and gestures.

- Keep your head up and look around you rather than gazing at the floor. Take an interest in your surroundings.

- Meet people's gaze and make eye contact.

- Smile.

Acting the part

First impressions

Greet the interviewer in a friendly, self-assured manner. He or she will be impressed and you will feel confident. Before you enter the room, take a moment to centre yourself. Stand tall, pull your shoulders back and head up. Take a slow, deep breath in and out. As you enter smile and make eye contact with the interviewer, and with anyone else in the room. Remember to close the door behind you.

When interviewers introduce themselves, say, 'Hello, very nice to meet you,' or 'Pleased to meet you,' and give a firm, even handshake. Sit down when invited to or, if the interviewer forgets, wait for a moment before asking 'May I sit down?' or 'Is it OK if I take a seat?'

Let the interviewer take the initiative and be ready to respond appropriately. Be alert to his or her behaviour and follow his or her lead. Remember, this is the interviewer's territory, so don't attempt to dominate it. Wait before shaking hands and sitting down so that the interviewer can take the lead and remain in control. It's not just politeness, it's essential psychology.

Maintaining the image

Build on that good first impression throughout the interview. Use body language to appear confident, reliable, enthusiastic, responsive and energetic, as well as interested and intelligent. Appear alert and relaxed, and avoid nervous mannerisms: crossing your legs, folding your arms, fidgeting, tapping or nail-biting:

- Don't perch nervously on the edge of your chair. Sit well back in it.

- Sit upright with both feet on the floor and your hands resting in your lap or on the arms of the chair.

- Keep your head up and look at the interviewer. Lean forward slightly in a listening position.

- Maintain good eye contact. Vary your gaze and avoid a fixed stare by looking all around the interviewer's face: mouth, cheeks and brow as well.

- Nod intelligently when the interviewer asks you questions or explains something.

- Remember to smile, warmly and naturally rather than keeping a fixed grin.

- As you relax, you can let your natural gestures emphasize points and show more of your character.

If you feel yourself getting tired or losing energy, sit upright, breathe in and concentrate on your posture, gestures and facial expression all being up and open. This should make you look and feel alert again. On the other hand, if nerves threaten to get the better of you, glance away for a moment, breathe deeply from your stomach, relax your shoulders and let your hands rest on your lap. You will just look as if you are thinking, and you can continue your answer with renewed confidence.

Lasting impressions

Always leave a good impression behind you. Final impressions are nearly as important as first ones, and will colour the interviewer's image of you when he or she recalls the interview later. Be alert to 'winding up' signals from your interviewer. He or she might say something like 'We'll be in touch early next week,' and thank you for coming to be interviewed. Make eye contact, smile, shake hands and thank the interviewer for seeing you. Say something like 'It's been very nice meeting you, I look forward to hearing from you soon,' or 'It's been a very interesting afternoon, I look forward to your decision.' Then leave confidently and decisively. Don't hang around waiting to be told what to do.

The interview isn't over until you are out of the building. Wait until you are well away before loosening your tie, rummaging in your handbag, or if you really must, lighting a cigarette. The same applies to any time you spend on the company's premises – check Debbie MacEke's expert quote at the end of this chapter.

Overcoming nerves

Although everyone dreads interview nerves, interviewers are often sympathetic and prepared to make allowances for them. They are not going to rule you out just because you seem a bit jittery at first. If your nerves persist throughout the interview, though, they will start worrying how you cope with stress. And if nerves stop you giving proper answers, they will never find out what you can do. Don't fear nerves, but don't let them prevent you from making a good impression either. Thorough preparation will improve your confidence. You will know what the organization wants, understand why you are right for the job and know how, where and when you have demonstrated the competencies needed.

Rehearse your interview skills beforehand. Practise entering a room, shaking hands and so on, until you can do them smoothly and confidently. Rehearse your answers to interview questions, too, so that they feel familiar. Make sure you are organized before the interview so you can anticipate and avoid unexpected setbacks. Make sure, for example, that you know exactly where the interview is and how to get there. Double-check the date, time and name of the person you are meeting. Get everything ready the night before, including:

- a copy of your CV or application form;
- name, address and phone number of the company;
- fully charged mobile in case of accidents or delays;

- car keys or money for fares;

- any other documents or equipment you need for the interview.

It's a good idea to avoid tea and coffee for an hour or so before the interview. Caffeine can make you jittery, and any drink has a stimulating effect on the bladder, especially when you are nervous. Avoid alcohol altogether. You will need all your wits about you.

When you arrive at the place where the interview is being held, find a cloakroom and check your appearance thoroughly: hair, teeth, make-up, buttons and zips, hems, and any runs or snags in tights. Do a quick relaxation exercise to get your nerves under control:

- Shrug your shoulders and swing your arms to relax them.

- Take a slow breath in to the count of three.

- Hold your breath for the count of three.

- Breathe out slowly to the count of five.

- Take a breath in to the count of five.

- Hold your breath for the count of five.

- Breathe out to the count of seven.

- Breathe normally.

Nerves can make you tense up physically: hunch your shoulders, fold your arms, cross your legs and lower your head. Take a moment at the beginning of the interview to consciously open up. Hold your head up, put your shoulders back, your feet on the floor and hands on your lap or the arms of the chair. Breathe in deeply and answer the first question.

EXPERT QUOTE

Attitude is important. Things like interest, commitment and pride in one's work need to come over in the interview.

MAGGIE FELLOWS, PROJECT MANAGER, SOUTH WEST TUC

EXPERT QUOTE

The interview starts in the reception area. Companies can and do ask receptionists what they think of candidates and the impression they made when they arrived. Were they polite, were they friendly? You could even say it starts in the car park. Don't park in the managing director's space, for example.

DEBBIE MACEKE, RESOURCE CENTRE MANAGER, ROLLS-ROYCE

16
Answering interview questions

This chapter looks at answering the questions nearly everybody gets asked at interviews. The next chapter discusses job-specific questions in more detail, while this one considers general questions as well as looking at how to tackle the trickier ones and the ones you would rather not have to answer. It also gives suggestions about what to say when interviewers ask if you have any questions for them.

The three rules

There are three key rules when answering interview questions. They might sound obvious, but they are easily forgotten under stress. When you practise interview techniques with friends or family, keep these three things in mind:

- **Listen to the question and stick to the point when you answer it.**
  Don't go off at a tangent. Most people have a two-minute attention span, so keep your answers shorter than that.

- **Illustrate your answers with real-life examples.** Don't just say you can do x, y or z. Support your claim – see below for more about how to do this.

- **Don't waffle.** When you have answered the question, stop talking. Don't let silence draw you into irrelevancies. When you have finished, add something like 'I hope that answers your question,' then smile and wait for the next one.

In addition to the three rules above, imagine the words 'relevant to this job' after every question.

Illustrating your answers with real-life examples

A useful way to organize your examples and anecdotes about how you have used your skills and abilities, and to make sure you include all the relevant information that the interviewer needs, is to break them down into SAR headings:

- S – Situation. Briefly outline the situation that arose or that you found yourself in. Who or what was involved? What were the problems or considerations?

- A – Action. What did you do? What skills and abilities did you use?

- R – Result. What was the result of the action you took? What was the benefit to those involved? What did you learn from the experience?

By covering all these points in your preparation, you can make sure that you have all the information that you need to give a comprehensive account of your real-life skills and abilities without waffling or wandering from the point.

What sort of questions will they ask?

Most interviewers prepare two sets of questions for the interview, structured questions and person-specific questions. Structured questions are decided before the interview. Based on the job description, they examine how well each applicant meets the needs of the job. They include questions like 'What do you see as the main priorities of the job?' and 'Tell me about an occasion when you had to motivate a team member. How did you go about it?' They are usually the same for all candidates, and mean each applicant is matched against the job requirements rather than competing with each other. In contrast, the person-specific questions are based on your CV, and explore your specific circumstances more fully.

Questions they ask everybody

In the next chapter, we look at interview questions for different types of job. There are some questions, however, that get asked at most interviews. If you plan and practise your answers now, you will be ready. Even if the questions are not exactly the same or phrased a different way, you will be prepared enough to be flexible and answer with confidence.

'What experience do you have for this job?'

You will know from your preparation what the job requires and how well you match it. For example:

> I have x years' experience working in [*your relevant career background*], where my achievements include [*give relevant examples*]. My familiarity with [*a relevant process, piece of equipment or working environment, for example*] will allow me to contribute to the job from the start. I understand [*a key element from the job description that demonstrates you know what the job involves*], and the importance of [*another key skill or ability*]. These have been essential elements in my current job and I appreciate their importance. For example, [*give a short anecdote demonstrating your use of these skills*].

'How has your job changed since you have been there?'
'Do you have more responsibilities now than when you started?'
'Have your responsibilities increased while you have been doing your current job?'

Emphasize that you are flexible and adapt easily to change. Tell them about the changes that have happened in your job including different working methods, different tasks and different management styles. Include extra tasks or responsibilities you have taken on, and especially any promotion you have received. You have probably taken on more as you have become familiar with the job and more confident, even if your responsibilities have not increased officially. For example:

> My responsibilities have increased significantly. When I first started, my supervisor [*manager, boss*] instructed me about every job and checked my work at each stage. It meant I learnt how to do the job thoroughly, and how to work efficiently and to a high standard. As I became more confident about what I was doing, I took responsibility for [*your relevant duties*]. These days, my supervisor gives me the work schedule and I plan the work order and carry it out [*for example*]. I believe the confidence my supervisor shows in my ability demonstrates how I've developed in the job, and that I'm ready to take on greater responsibility.

'What has your current job taught you?'

'What did you learn from your last job?'

Interviewers like to see that you are learning and developing. Consider:

- the personal qualities you have developed;

- responsibilities you have taken on;

- practical skills you have developed.

For example:

> I'm always willing to learn and my current position has taught me a number of things. I've developed [*a skill or ability*] through [*a responsibility or role you took on*]. I would also say that I've learned the importance of [*a relevant skill or personal quality you learnt the value of and developed further as a result*]. For example, [*give a couple of brief anecdotes showing these competencies in action*].

'Do you prefer working alone or with others?'

Tailor your answer to the job description. As there are times in most jobs when you have to do both, however, reassure the interviewer that you are flexible and would be happy in either role. For example:

> I've worked as a team member in [*give a specific situation*], and I've worked on my own in [*give another situation*]. I'm happy to do either depending on the requirements of the job. I've found, though, that working in [*whichever the job requires*] allows me to [*give some positive benefits*].

'What makes a good team member?'

'How well do you work in a team?'

The interviewer will ask this because the job requires teamwork. Reply that you work very well in a team, base your answer on the following qualities, and give examples of how you have demonstrated them. Good team members are:

- communicative;

- supportive of the other members;

- flexible – they fit in with others and adapt to changing demands;

- unselfish – they put the needs of the other team members on a level with their own;

- interested in the success of the team as a whole, not just their own performance.

For example:

> From past experience, I know I enjoy being part of a team, I like the camaraderie and that feeling of all working together towards a common goal [*for example*]. I believe a good team member should be [*choose from the list above*] and I try to demonstrate these qualities when working with others. For example, in my last job, [*give your example of working well in a team, demonstrating at least one key quality from the list*].

'Why do you want to change jobs?'

'What were your reasons for leaving your last job?'

Have a positive answer ready. Good reasons for changing your job include:

- **opportunity**: the chance to develop or do something new;

- **challenge**: more demanding responsibilities;

- **promotion**: the job you are applying for is a step up from your current one;

- **money**: your salary no longer reflects your value;

- **reputation**: applying to a more prestigious company;

- **security**: a more secure job with a more stable company (as long as 'challenge and ambition' weren't key words in the job ad);

- **location**: the company you are applying to is in a better or more convenient place (a useful extra, but try not to make it your main reason).

Start by saying that you enjoy your current job and explain why, despite that, you want to change. For example:

> I've enjoyed working [*in your current job*], especially the opportunity they have given me to [*mention something you have achieved*]. Unfortunately, it's a small company and there's no opportunity for advancement with it in the near future [*for example – the promotion reason*].

Another example:

> I enjoy working [*in your current job*], and I've particularly appreciated [*mention a few key points*]. However, since developing my bookkeeping skills [*for example*] over the past year,

I now find this side of the job more appealing. Unfortunately, a suitable position using these skills is unlikely to arise in the near future so I'm looking for a post where I can develop them more fully [*the opportunity reason*]. I believe this job offers just such an opportunity.

'Why do you want to work here?'

'What interests you most about this job?'

Think about what you can give, rather than what you hope to get. Concentrate on things that mean you can work at your best: conditions, management methods, opportunities, challenges, the company structure, reputation and so on. Tell the interviewer about the positive things you can contribute under those conditions. Some examples:

I'm looking for a position where I can use my [*relevant skill or area of experience*] to the full. I believe this job provides that opportunity. I also see it as a natural development from [*your experience, further qualifications or training, etc*].

I believe [*company name*] provides a challenging, stimulating and supportive environment for its employees [*for example*]. I have x years' experience in [*your field of work*] and have [*mention a couple of achievements*]. I'm looking for the opportunity to continue to achieve at that level and beyond, in a company that will help me develop professionally. I believe your company offers just such an opportunity.

I've enjoyed working in [*your current job*], especially [*mention a key feature*], but it's a small company and unfortunately there's no opportunity for advancement in the near future [*for example*]. I believe an expanding company [*for example*] such as yours offers a greater range of challenges and opportunities, in particular [*a key responsibility or skill mentioned in the job description that you want to develop further*].

'Tell me about yourself.'

This is such an open question that it's difficult to know where to start. The interviewer wants to know about your:

- current job;
- background, education and training;
- skills and strengths that make you good at the job;
- experience and accomplishments;
- attraction to your particular field and how you got into it;

- high points of your career so far;

- goals for the future.

For example:

> I am a [*give a brief description*]. I'm an experienced [*major aspect of the job*] with an extensive knowledge of [*relevant knowledge area*] including [*a key point*]. My main skills [*or qualifications*] are [*two or three key ones*].
>
> I also have experience in [*your next most relevant skill or knowledge*], including [*develop one or two key points*].
>
> My achievements include [*two or three major achievements*]. The benefits to my current employer have been [*outline the benefits – what you have increased, decreased or improved*]. I believe the position you're offering would allow me to [*what you want to do or develop*].

After you have answered the question, the interviewer may go on to ask you to fill in more details: 'Tell me more about X,' or 'Can you say a bit more about Y?' Answer, bearing in mind the relevance to the job, and supply anecdotes to illustrate and support what you say.

Dealing with negative questions

Sometimes interviewers ask rather negative questions, such as:

- 'What do you dislike about your current job?'

- 'What did you dislike about your last boss?'

- 'What sort of things do colleagues do that really irritate you?'

They are not interested in what you disliked, but in whether you are a complainer. Just smile and give a neutral answer.

'What do you dislike about your current job?'
'What appeals to you least about this job?'

You could say, for example:

> I think [*a routine task everyone dislikes – form filling, filing, record-keeping, etc*] is probably the least demanding part of my work. However, it's one of my responsibilities and important to

the job as a whole, so I get it done as quickly and efficiently as I can, which allows me to attend to the more rewarding aspects of the job.

'What do you think your last boss could have done better?'

'What did you dislike about your boss/supervisor?'

A possible answer is:

> I always found X a very good employer/supervisor. I believe he/she gave me the best guidance possible, and the opportunity to develop my career to the point where I'm ready for the challenges this new job presents.

Another sort of negative question invites you to criticize yourself. These are questions like:

- 'What is your greatest weakness?'
- 'What do you find most difficult to deal with in yourself?'
- 'What would you change about yourself if you could?'

Interviewers are not concerned with your weaknesses; they are interested in how you react to criticism, a key factor in how easy you will be to work with in future. Rather than give an answer that reveals damaging weaknesses, or claiming improbably to have no imperfections, try one of the following tactics:

- Describe a 'flaw' most people would see as a strength.
- Give a humorous flaw most people would sympathize with.
- Describe a weakness you have overcome.
- Offer a weakness that will have no impact on the job you are applying for.

'What is your greatest weakness?'

Good answers include:

> I'm a bit of a perfectionist. I won't rest if I know something isn't right.

> I've been accused of being a workaholic because I can't relax while there's something that needs doing.

Last year, I would have said speaking in public and giving presentations, but since I went on a course to improve my skills it's no longer a problem.

I used to have difficulty keeping up with all the filing the job entails. I've learnt from bitter experience to do it first thing in the morning so I'm free to concentrate on more demanding responsibilities.

Questions about salary

How do you deal with questions about salary? The problem is, if you name a figure you could either be under-selling yourself or pricing yourself out of the market. Avoid the issue until the organization offers you a job. A job offer should not depend on the salary you are prepared to accept; the job should be offered first and the salary stated. It's up to you to accept or reject the offer, or negotiate around it.

Get some idea of what the job is worth beforehand. Find out whether:

- the organization has a fixed pay scale;

- there are ads for similar jobs where the salary is stated;

- there are salary surveys for your profession you could refer to;

- there are perks that would add to your total salary package;

- there's someone in a similar job you could speak to (don't ask bluntly what his or her salary is, just ask what someone like you might expect to get).

'What is your current salary?'

You could reply:

It would be misleading if I gave you a bald figure. My salary is part of a much wider package that takes into consideration [*whatever else you receive – overtime pay, bonuses, perks, discounts, pension contributions, company car, staff facilities, etc*]. I could prepare an accurate figure if we need to talk about it in more detail [*when they offer you the job, for example*].

'We're offering around £20,000. How does that sound to you?'

'What sort of salary are you expecting?'

'What do you think you're worth?'

If you say £20,000 sounds fine, that's what you'll get, rather than the £23,000 the organization might have gone up to. Say, for example:

> I believe current salaries for this sort of job are around that figure, up to £25,000.

> I believe this sort of job attracts a salary of around £20,000–25,000. Bearing in mind my qualifications and experience, I would expect to be at the higher rather than the lower end of that range.

Dealing with closed questions

Interviewers *should* ask open questions that you can respond to with examples of your past competence and experience. Examples of open questions are:

- What do you like about your current job?

- How do you get on with your colleagues?

- What would you say are the key skills for a manager?

In contrast, closed questions are those you can answer with a simple 'Yes' or 'No':

- Do you like your current job?

- Do you get on with your colleagues?

- Is leadership a key skill for a manager?

Treat closed questions as if they were open ones. Say 'Yes' or 'No' as appropriate, then give more information.

'Do you think communication skills are important in this sort of job?'

Say, for example:

> I believe communication skills are very important in this job. If I may give an example, in my last position [*give a SAR-based example of when this skill was valuable*].

'Do you like your current job?'

Answer, for example:

> Yes, I like my current job. I particularly like [*something relevant to the new job*]. However, I believe that the position you are offering will allow me to [*develop in a specific direction and use relevant skills and aptitudes*].

Dealing with the person-specific questions

Having read your CV, the interviewer will want to probe into details. He or she will want to know more about:

- very good matches with the job requirements;
- specific details about past jobs: tasks, responsibilities and achievements;
- poor matches with the job requirements;
- being under- or over-qualified for the post;
- any gaps in employment;
- frequent job changes;
- reasons for leaving jobs;
- unusual career moves.

A useful way to answer difficult questions is:

- agree with the interviewer: if he or she thinks there's a problem, don't argue;
- appreciate his or her point of view; but then say, 'However...';
- give reasons, explanations or mitigating circumstances that help your case;
- underline how much you have changed since then;
- confirm the problem won't affect the organization.

'You've been out of work a long time.'

'You've had some unusual career moves.'

'You're rather over-qualified for this job.'

Reply, for example:

> Yes, [*I have been out of work a long time, had some unusual career moves, appear over-qualified*], and I understand your concern that [*I might be out of practice, uncertain of my career path, get bored and move on*]. However, [*go through any reasons or explanations*], and [*give an example of how you have changed or how this situation is different*]. So, although I understand why you are bringing the matter up, I can assure you it's [*not a problem that's going to affect you in this job*]. In fact, [*if possible, show what strengths, skills or experience you have gained as a result, and how that might benefit the company*].

'You were in your last job a long time. How do you think you'll adjust to a new post?'

Reassure the interviewer you are not lacking ambition and initiative. If there were reasons you stayed so long, tell him or her. Maybe it was the only suitable job in the area, or you felt loyal to a small firm. Explain that the job was always changing and there were always new challenges. You could also say you worked on several different projects where you had to be adaptable and flexible. Give some examples and anecdotes to support that.

'You were in your last job for x years. Why weren't you promoted in that time?'

Give reasons: it was a small company, or you were top of your field with nowhere to go, for example. Outline what you learnt and what you achieved, and emphasize how your responsibilities increased even though there was not a formal promotion. Explain that lack of opportunity is the reason you are currently looking for a new job.

'You've been in your current job a rather short time. Why are you changing so soon?'

Acceptable reasons might be:

- redundancy or reorganization;

- relocation – yours or the company's;

- it was a short-term contract or temporary job;
- it was always intended as a stopgap while you looked for another more suitable post;
- a genuine mistake – the job wasn't what you thought it was going to be;
- an unforeseen change of circumstances – you need full-time work rather than part-time or vice versa, for example;
- this new job was too good an opportunity to miss.

'You seem to have changed jobs frequently. Is there a reason for that?'

Reassure the interviewer that you won't move again in a few months. Emphasize your commitment and intention to stay. Explain if previous companies have closed down, reorganized or relocated. If past jobs were short-term contract or temporary, change your CV so temp jobs come under one heading and it doesn't look as if you are job-hopping.

If necessary, explain that you have made some bad career choices, because of youthful inexperience, perhaps, but are now ready to settle down to long-term career commitments. Say how and why you have changed, and show how the experience you have gained will be of value in this new job.

'You've had some very different jobs.'

'This job is rather different from your current one.'

Reassure the interviewer that what seem like random job choices actually make sense. Most people have natural aptitudes and preferences, so it isn't as difficult as it sounds. Perhaps they all use problem-solving skills or interpersonal skills. Maybe they all require organization or creativity. Demonstrate how each job relates to the others, what they have in common, and how the skills you have learnt will be relevant and useful in the new job.

'It's a long time since your last job.'

The interviewer may be wondering why no one has employed you yet. Give good reasons for your period of unemployment. If you had an offer that fell through, tell the interviewer, unless it was due to a bad reference or something similar. If you were made redundant, tell the interviewer you needed time to think about your career rather than just take anything going. You could also explain how your redundancy package allowed you to fulfil a dream such as travelling, but that you are ready to settle down again now.

You might also say that at this stage in your career, you want to make the best use of your skills and experience and have been very selective about who you have applied to. Show how you have used the time to update and upgrade your skills through training or study.

'What have you been doing since your last job?'

Include things that make your days sound structured and full of activity:

- Updating your skills. Include any courses of study or training you have done.

- Vocational interests you have become involved with or had more time to develop.

- Voluntary work you have done.

- Emphasize the organized approach you took to job hunting itself – the research, networking and so on involved.

'There are quite long gaps in your record. Is there a reason for that?'

The interviewer might be worried that there are underlying reasons – perhaps drug use, ill health or family problems – that would be an ongoing problem. Explain the gaps as well as you can, and stress your eagerness to settle down and get on with your career.

If the gaps were caused by major problems, explain that they are in the past, your life has changed for the better, and clarify how and why. Convince the interviewer that they will in no way affect your ability to work effectively for the organization, and give an example of your current commitment and drive. Demonstrate how overcoming your problem has strengthened and matured you, and how you can use that in the job.

'Your last job seems a bit of a step down. Was there a reason for that?'

'Isn't this job a bit of a backwards/sideways step for you?'

Show how the job fits your career plan. Maybe you took a sideways step to develop new skills or to consolidate them. Perhaps you undertook training but also needed hands-on experience, or you reached the top in one field and wanted to use your skills and experience in a different environment. Perhaps you are downshifting, taking a less stressful, time-consuming job because you have other priorities. Show how your expertise will be a benefit in this job, and don't let the interviewer feel it's a soft option or the last step before retirement.

'Do you feel you're over-qualified/experienced for this position?'

The interviewer could be worried you will get a better offer, or that you won't take orders from a younger, less-qualified manager. Assure him or her you wouldn't have applied if you didn't think you were right for the job. Say what interests you about it, and how your experience will benefit the company.

If you think the interviewer is hinting you are too old, point out the benefits age brings:

- You are mature, which means you are reliable, professional, prudent and responsible.

- You have encountered and resolved many problems.

- You have learnt to get on with people in most situations.

- You have realistic expectations of life, work and your colleagues.

- You have abundant skills and experience the organization could benefit from.

- You have a record of commitment and dependability.

- You have a proven track record of achievement and success.

- You survived the technological and employment revolutions of the past couple of decades. You are resilient, flexible and adaptable.

'Do you feel your lack of practical experience could be a problem?'

If you are newly qualified, show you understand how your theoretical knowledge applies in practice. Demonstrate how quickly you learn practical things, giving past examples of this ability. Emphasize practical experience gained in other life areas and show how it applies to this job.

'Do you feel your lack of qualifications could be a problem?'

Focus attention on how your practical experience, skill and expertise will be of value. If you will be working with people more qualified than you, give a couple of brief anecdotes showing how you have gained respect and cooperation in similar circumstances in the past.

Inappropriate and illegal questions

Employment law actively discourages discrimination, so you should not have to answer questions about:

- marital status, number or ages of children;
- nationality, race, ethnicity or religion;
- gender or sexual orientation;
- disabilities or handicaps;
- political affiliation or membership of legal organizations;
- age;
- financial status;
- spent convictions.

However, this is a complex area. There can be exemptions on specific grounds – a need for female care workers, for example, might justify gender discrimination – and you can be asked about anything that has a direct effect on your ability to do the job. You should not be asked general questions about disability, for example, but the interviewer can ask whether you are able to stand for specified periods of time, should that be required in the post.

If the interviewer asks an illicit question, you are entitled to say that you don't think the question is relevant and refuse to answer. That could leave both you and the interviewer feeling embarrassed, however, and sap your confidence for the rest of the interview.

Assess the situation and the interviewer. He or she might be trying to show interest or sympathy rather than discrimination. If you wish, you can ignore the inappropriateness of the question and treat it like any other. Either allay his or her fears – 'I understand this job involves a significant amount of [travel, lifting, shift work, etc] and I can assure you that my [family responsibilities, disability, childcare arrangements, marriage plans, etc] will in no way interfere with my ability to do that' – or give a non-committal answer – 'I can assure you there is nothing [about my religion, politics, family responsibility, age, whatever] that will affect my performance in this job.'

If you feel the question is more deliberate, you could refer it back to the interviewer, saying for example, 'I'm not quite sure how that question relates to my ability to do the job. Could you clarify for me?' If the interviewer knows the question is illegal, he or she will move swiftly on.

Your questions to the interviewer

Towards the end of the interview, interviewers will ask if you have any questions for them. Avoid asking about things like salary, hours and holiday entitlements. Prepare two or three questions that show your interest in the job and the company, such as questions about:

- **the job itself**: responsibilities, appraisal methods, departmental organization;

- **opportunities**: travel, training, promotion opportunities;

- **the company**: expectations, growth and development.

Don't ask things you should know from the job specification, but you can ask for clarification or more information. For example:

What would be the priorities in this job for the first six months?

Do you offer opportunities for training and development?

What are the biggest challenges facing the team/department currently?

May I ask why the job has become vacant?

What would my career prospects be with the company?

If I were to join this company, where would you see me in five years' time?

Do you promote internally?

What are the company's development plans in [an area you're interested in]?

How does the company see the job developing over the next few years?

I'm very interested in this job and I believe I could do it well. May I ask if you have any reservations about my suitability?

EXPERT QUOTE

Convince them you can do what you say you can. Give actual evidence: 'For example, when working in my job as a...'

MAGGIE FELLOWS, PROJECT MANAGER, SOUTH WEST TUC

EXPERT QUOTE

I do need to know what people's weaknesses are so I will probe. I want to know what people have learnt from setbacks and what they would do differently in the future as a result. As long as people can learn from their mistakes, that's fine.

TINA BUCHANAN, GROUP DIRECTOR, HAMWORTHY ENGINEERING

17
Questions for specific jobs

This chapter focuses on specific questions for specific sorts of jobs. Different jobs require different skills, and the questions interviewers ask take these differences into account. The interviewer is likely to decide on six or seven key competencies necessary for the job and ask you questions about times you have demonstrated each of them:

'Tell me about a time you demonstrated y.'
'Give me an example of when you've done x.'

Remember to keep your answers SAR-based:

- Situation

- Action

- Result

He or she will follow up with questions to clarify points or draw out more detail from you:

'What were the circumstances surrounding that event?'

'What difficulties did you encounter; how did you deal with them?'

'What was the eventual outcome?'

'Is there anything, with hindsight, you would have done differently?'

The chapter is divided into different job areas:

Find the section most like the sort of work you do, read the questions and decide how you would answer them. Preparing the answers will help you sort out key points and increase your confidence, even though the questions you get in the interview are unlikely to be exactly the same.

Questions for practical jobs

The interviewer is trying to discover whether you can do the job competently and dependably. As with your CV, the key question he or she wants answered is, 'Are you reliable?' Refer back to Chapter 8, 'CVs for specific jobs', for more ideas about what this means in practice. Demonstrate clearly that you know what needs to be done and how to do it. When going through the questions and preparing your answers, focus on:

- Your practical experience: the responsibilities you have had, the tasks you have done and the skills you have developed.
- Your key skills: practical skills that have proved useful. If you have specific qualifications or training, include them in your answers.
- Your personal qualities. Include your:
  - competence and dependability;
  - self-reliance and flexibility;
  - ability to follow instructions accurately and find out further information where necessary;
  - any qualities that have proved useful in your job – patience, for example.

Keep these points in mind when thinking about your answers to interview questions. Stick to three or four key points and put them across strongly.

'What are your greatest strengths?'
'What are your best qualities?'
'What makes you a good [what your job is]?'

Focus on your practical strengths, your experience and your reliability. Give examples of how, where and when you have demonstrated these qualities. For example:

> I believe my greatest strengths with regard to this job are my experience, my reliability, and my [a relevant skill]. I've been working in [your relevant background] for x years and my knowledge of [relevant area] and familiarity with [relevant process or equipment] mean I can do the job competently and efficiently. I believe my current employer would agree that I can be relied on to do the job even under difficulties/pressure. For example, [describe a time you did that].

'Are you reliable?'

Illustrate your answer with an example of how dependable you are. For example:

> I believe I am, and I think my present employer would agree. I have an excellent timekeeping and attendance record, and I take my responsibilities seriously, completing [your tasks] on time and to a high standard. It's important to me that I do a good job even when it takes extra effort. For example, [give an example of when you had to overcome a problem to get a job done, and the resulting benefit to the company].

'What are some of the problems you encounter in your job?'
'Tell me about a problem you've had to deal with.'

Give an example of a practical problem and include the following points in your answer:

- You stayed calm.
- You were clear-headed.
- Experience and common sense helped you find the solution.
- You kept your supervisor/manager informed.

For example:

> In [*your job*] common difficulties include [*practical difficulties such as breakdowns, malfunctions, hold-ups, etc*]. My supervisor relies on me to sort out everyday problems. For example, [*give an example of how you resolved one of these problems*]. On another occasion, [*give an example of how you saw a problem coming and took steps to prevent it*].

'Do you get bored doing routine work?'

Most practical jobs have their routine side, so reply that you don't get bored. You have a methodical approach to things and enjoy doing a thorough job. However, you can be flexible when the job requires – outline some of the challenges you've risen to in the past.

'Have you ever worked without supervision?'

'What qualities do you need to work unsupervised?'

The interviewer wants to know if you can:

- take responsibility for your work;
- get on with the job without someone looking over your shoulder;
- solve everyday problems;
- take action in everyday situations;
- make appropriate decisions.

Say, for example:

> I often work alone without direct supervision because [*explain why – you work off-site; you have no direct line manager; etc*]. I consult [*whoever you consult*] when there's a technical problem [*or anything outside your responsibility*], but otherwise, I plan my own work and handle everyday problems and decisions myself. For example, [*give an example*].

'Have you ever had problems with supervisors?'

Say you have never had any problems. Supervisors see that the job gets done, and you understand that sometimes guidance and constructive criticism are required.

'Do you follow instructions well?'

Say, for example:

> Yes, I believe I do. Like most people, I prefer to be given reasons and explanations for things, and my current supervisor is very good about that. I make sure I've clarified the information before I carry out the task, and I feed back the results to my supervisor afterwards if necessary. For example, [*give an example of a time you did that*].

'What have you done that shows initiative?'

'How do you decide when to use your initiative and when to refer to your manager?'

'What kinds of decisions do you make independently in your current job?'

Can you balance following instructions with thinking for yourself? Try to show that you can act on your own initiative when the need arises, acting responsibly to resolve problems and make decisions. For example:

> My current company sets out clear guidelines about what decisions I can make and what options are practical [*you are used to making everyday decisions*]. It also has clear procedures for most circumstances [*you can understand and follow instructions*]. If a situation arose where there were no guidelines, it was urgent or I was unable to contact my supervisor, I would make a decision based on my experience of similar circumstances. I'd keep a record of my actions and inform my manager as soon as possible. For example, [*tell the interviewer about a time when you did that*].

'Which is more important, speed or accuracy?'

You need to show that you can be both fast *and* accurate. For example:

> I believe they're both important; I try to manage my workload so that I achieve both. Fortunately, my experience means I'm able to work to a high speed while maintaining quality.

'What are your views on health and safety?'

'Have you ever had to bend health and safety rules to get a job done?'

Practical jobs can involve working in dangerous conditions. The interviewer needs to see that you are aware of the importance of health and safety, know about issues relevant to your job, and understand and follow the regulations. Let the interviewer know if you have had any health and safety training.

Never ignore health and safety regulations at work. You should say that you never do so and you would not expect to be asked to. If you have found ways of improving health and safety, include that in your answer.

'What would you do if someone on your team wasn't pulling their weight?'

This is trying to find out if you can handle everyday problems yourself, and whether you know when to refer them on. Say, for example:

> It depends on the reason. If there were health and safety issues, if someone was drunk on the job for example, I would discuss it with the supervisor. If the person was just being lazy, I'd joke him out of it until he got the message [*for example*]. [*Tell the interviewer about a time when you successfully resolved a similar situation.*]

As well as the questions above, you will be asked specific things about your type of work. These are too individual to cover in detail, but you know what your work involves and should be able to anticipate what the questions will be. They will include things like:

- how you handle commonly occurring tasks;

- what you would do in various situations;

- your understanding of specific processes;

- how you would deal with situations that could arise;

- your experience of using particular machinery or equipment.

Give full, detailed answers based on your experience.

Questions for creative jobs

The interviewer is assessing whether you will use your skill, talent and expertise to provide solutions to problems. As with your CV, the key question is 'Will you deliver?' See Chapter 8, 'CVs for specific jobs', for what this means in practice. Demonstrate clearly that you will come up with innovative solutions, on time and to budget. When preparing your answers, focus on:

- **your career history**: the skills you have developed, the challenges you have overcome, and your experience of solving creative problems;

- **your key achievements**: understand your successes and be able to talk about them from both a technical and a creative viewpoint;

- **your key abilities**: your full range of skills and how they have contributed to your achievements.

The personal qualities the interviewer will be looking for include:

- self-motivation;

- innovation;

- flexibility;

- energy and enthusiasm;

- resilience;

- professionalism.

Keep these points in mind while you prepare your answers.

'What do you know about our company?'

Start with general comments – history, products and services, for example – then focus on your own area – product position or marketing strategy, for example. Tell the interviewer why the sector interests you and why working for the organization appeals to you.

'Why should I hire you?'

Reply that it is because you can provide first-rate creative solutions to the organization's problems. For example:

I can deliver [*first-rate copy, top-quality artwork, etc*] as shown by [*recap your key achievements*]. I have x years' experience working in [*your career background*], and I have/am [*recap your skills and experience*].

'What can you bring to this job?'

'What are your greatest strengths?'

'What are your outstanding qualities?'

'What makes you a good [what you do]?'

Emphasize your key strengths and talents, along with your achievements. For example:

I believe I can bring to this job [*key skill or quality*]. I am [*outline your key qualities*] and have [*your key skills and abilities*]. To date, I have [*give your achievements*]. In addition, I understand [*a relevant factor of the job*] which I believe would allow me to [*make a significant contribution to the company*]. Finally, I believe my current employer would agree that one of my key strengths is my ability to do the job even under difficult conditions. For example, [*describe a time you successfully completed a job to a high creative level under pressure*].

'What would you do if we gave you a completely free hand?'

You need to know the company, what it has done in the past and its intended future direction. Whatever you suggest, you must:

- outline your proposals clearly;

- explain why you would make the decisions you suggest;

- show how they would benefit the company.

'How do you keep pace with changes and innovations in your job?'

Include the following:

- professional associations;

- professional, trade and business magazines;

- courses and seminars;

- online professional groups;

- trade fairs, shows and exhibitions;

- suppliers and clients;

- business contacts.

For example:

> Keeping up with new [*products, ideas, trends, etc*] is important in this job. I [*say what you do to keep up*]. It takes a bit of commitment, but I believe it's essential. For example, [*give an example of how knowing something ahead of time benefited you, your job and the company*].

'What are the reasons for your professional success?'

If you just say you have been lucky, the interviewer might wonder what will happen when your luck runs out. If you give reasons based on real skills, it's likely you will continue to be successful. Base the reasons for your success on:

- creative skills you have developed;

- natural abilities you have built on and enhanced;

- the support you have received from others: colleagues, mentors and so on;

- your personal qualities and professional attitude;

- making good use of your opportunities.

'What's your attitude to challenge?'

Most creative people relish challenge and find it stimulates their best work. Make it clear that when you take on a challenge, you intend to succeed. Include examples of challenges you have met, and emphasize the benefit your success brought to the company.

'What is your attitude to risk?'

You want to appear adventurous, but not reckless. Unwise risk taking could cost the company money or prestige. Show that you can calculate risk. For example:

> Although I would never compromise the reputation of the company, most creative work entails taking risks from time to time. For example, [*give an example of a time you took a risk that paid*

off – how you analysed the risk, weighed the options, came to the decision it was worth it, kept your employer in the picture, and how the risk paid off – for the company and client as well as yourself]. On another occasion, however, [*give another brief anecdote about a time you came up with an innovative solution that avoided risk*].

'Would you say you were innovative?'

Give anecdotes demonstrating your flair for new ideas, how you made them work-able, how they were successful, and their benefit to the company.

'How well do you interact with people at different levels?'

You could be working with people with different needs. Perhaps you are a designer with production staff, management and clients to take into consideration, for exam-ple. Show you can communicate effectively with everyone involved while still putting your own views across. For example:

> I haven't experienced any problems in my current job. I work with [*the different groups you deal with*] and I [*outline what you do – presentations, discussions, reports, and at what level – departmental, board, client*]. For example, [*give an example that shows you communicating confidently and effectively with people at different levels of the company hierarchy*].

'Are you sensitive to criticism?'

'Describe a situation where your work was criticized. How did you respond?'

Show that you are able to take criticism but stand up for your ideas, too. For example:

> I'm mature enough to handle constructive criticism. I think it's essential if I want to continue to improve my performance. I remember early in my career, [*describe the event and how it arose. Who did the criticizing?*]. I listened to what she said and [*when the circumstances were explained*] I could see she had a point. We discussed it and [*describe how you came to a mutually agreeable solution*]. I learnt that [*something useful*].

'Describe a problem you have had to deal with. How did you handle it?'

Choose a creative problem and describe the skills and talents you used to overcome it creatively. Avoid problems that involve clashes with other people.

'Have you done the best work you are capable of doing?'

If you say 'No', the interviewer will wonder why not. Say 'Yes', and he or she might think you have nothing more to offer. Tell the interviewer you have done some terrific work in the past, but the job you are applying for offers the opportunity to do even better. For example:

> I've done some very good work, [*recap your achievements*] but [*the conditions in your organization*] would give me the opportunity to do even more [*specify what and how*].

'What are you like with deadlines?'

Missed deadlines mean lost reputation, lost clients and lost money, so you must say you would never miss one. Include anecdotes that show your determination to meet tight deadlines.

You will also be asked questions about specific aspects of your work and professional knowledge. These are highly specialized, but you know what your job entails, and can predict they will include things like:

- details of specific campaigns or projects: how you prepared, the issues involved, how you overcame problems, the reasons for your creative decisions, and so on;

- how you approach tasks and responsibilities;

- your understanding of specific processes;

- your experience using particular equipment, specialist programmes, etc;

- how you deal with actual problems and situations likely to arise in your occupation.

Base your answers on your experience, and let your interest and enthusiasm for your job shine through.

Questions for clerical jobs

The interviewer is trying to assess whether you can take on the job with the minimum of disruption. As with your CV, the key question interviewers want answered is 'Are you efficient?' Refer back to Chapter 8, 'CVs for specific jobs', for more ideas about what this means in practice.

When you are preparing for interview, make sure you thoroughly review your:

- key skills: word-processing, language or bookkeeping skills, use of software, familiarity with specific equipment, and knowledge of specific processes;

- key experience: the experience and knowledge that mean you know the job thoroughly and efficiently;

- any experience in roles such as supervision or planning, which are useful in most positions.

Keep these points in mind while working through the questions.

'What are your greatest strengths?'

'What can you bring to this job?'

'What makes you a good [what your job is]?'

The answer is your efficiency. Concentrate on that and add details of what it means:

- proficiency in specific skills and processes;

- a professional approach;

- organizational skills;

- competence and resourcefulness;

- experience.

Say, for example:

I would say my efficiency is my greatest strength. I have x years' experience in [*a relevant area*] and am highly proficient at [*your skills*]. These together with my [*professional qualities that help you do your job well*] ensure that I can do my job competently and professionally. For example, [*give a brief example of your efficiency and the benefit to the company*].

'Why should I hire you?'

The answer is, because you can take over the job smoothly and efficiently with as little disruption as possible. Say, for example:

> I have x years' experience working in [*your relevant experience*] and my familiarity with [*a relevant process, professional area, etc*] means I can pick up the job quickly and make a significant contribution from the start.

'Have you ever worked without supervision?'

'What qualities do you need to work unsupervised?'

See the answer to these questions given in 'Questions for practical jobs' (page 189).

'Have you ever had any problems with supervisors?'

See the answer given in 'Questions for practical jobs' (page 189).

'What have you done that shows initiative?'

'How do you decide when to use your initiative and when to refer to your supervisor/manager?'

'What kinds of decisions do you make in your current job?'

See the answer given in 'Questions for practical jobs' (page 190).

'What are some of the problems you encounter in your job?'

'Describe a difficult problem you have had to deal with.'

See the answer given in 'Questions for practical jobs' (page 188).

'Would you say you are reliable?'

See the answer given in 'Questions for practical jobs' (page 188).

'Which is more important, speed or accuracy?'

See the answer given in 'Questions for practical jobs' (page 190).

'Do you like analytical tasks?'

'Do you like doing detailed work?'

Give a positive answer. For example:

> I enjoy analytical tasks. I believe I have [*personal qualities: an eye for detail, patience,*
> *methodical approach, numerical aptitude, etc*] necessary for the task, and I've developed this by
> [*say how: qualifications, training, experience, etc*]. I believe they are valuable skills, [*give a brief*
> *example of a time your analytical skills were of benefit to the company*]. My decision to apply
> for this job is [*to some extent, to a large degree*] influenced by the chance to do more of this
> kind of work.

Another example:

> I enjoy doing detailed work. I have a methodical approach and can do that sort of work
> thoroughly and efficiently. I believe I also have [*useful qualities: eye for detail, patience,*
> *logical approach*] necessary for the task and have used these skills [*say how and where you*
> *have successfully done detailed work, whether in your job or some other capacity*].

'Do you prefer routine tasks and regular hours?'

'Do you get bored doing routine work?'

Routine work and regular hours are normal for clerical and administrative jobs.
However, saying you prefer them suggests you will complain when you have to work
extra hours or carry out non-routine tasks. Your answer needs to strike a balance.
For example:

> I appreciate that [*the job you're applying for*] largely entails routine work. I'm used to that,
> and luckily I have a methodical approach and can do routine jobs thoroughly and efficiently.
> However, there have been times, as in all jobs, when the work has been far from routine and
> the hours very irregular. I'm sure my current employer would agree that I've risen to those
> occasions and met the demands efficiently and effectively. For example, [*tell them about*
> *a time you've done so*].

'Would you say you were organized?'

You have to be organized for administrative work. Back up your claim with a couple
of examples illustrating your organizing skills and naturally organized nature.

'Do you work well under pressure?'

Demonstrate how well you have worked under pressure in the past. For example:

> I believe my supervisor/manager would agree that I work well under pressure. I've faced [*mention some situations such as urgent tasks, unexpected events, limited resources, short notice, etc*]. My priorities in a stressful situation are to stay calm, assess the situation and the resources available to me, decide the best course of action and act promptly and efficiently [*or whatever works for you*]. I've found that pressure can reveal unexpected strengths and success in such circumstances brings a lot of satisfaction. For example, [*illustrate with a brief anecdote*].

'What would you do if a chatty colleague was interrupting your work?'

The interviewer is asking if you can handle minor problems without disrupting your work, causing offence or involving management in minor personal irritations. Say, for example:

> I'd probably smile and say I was sorry but I was up to my eyes at the moment, and why didn't we meet for coffee during the break [*or whatever suits your own personal style*]. I had a similar problem a little while ago [*say what you did to resolve it tactfully*].

As well as these questions, you will be asked about practical aspects of your job and your professional knowledge. It's not possible to cover such highly specialized questions here, but you should be able to foresee what will be asked from your own experience. They will include:

- how you deal with specific circumstances that arise in the job;
- how you approach everyday tasks;
- your understanding of the responsibilities of the job;
- your areas of experience in detail;
- your knowledge of specific processes;
- your experience of using different software, etc;
- your experience of using particular pieces of equipment.

Give full, detailed, knowledgeable answers based on your experience.

Questions for sales and marketing jobs

The key question the interviewer wants answered is 'Can you sell?' (See Chapter 8, 'CVs for specific jobs'.) The best way to answer is by highlighting your previous sales success, so when preparing, thoroughly review your key achievements. Have plenty of examples illustrating your achievements. Put facts and figures to your successes, emphasizing your benefit to the company. Also review your career history. Remind yourself of the areas you have covered in the past and the sort of experience you have had. Think about these things as you answer the following questions.

'What do you know about our company?'

You need to know a lot, especially about its markets and products. As well as getting a broader perspective from the company website, company report or similar, read any catalogues or product guides. Think about why the company and its product or service interest you, and why you want to work for it.

'What do you think the key trends in the industry are?'

Read the trade journals and marketing magazines as well as newspapers. Outline the key trends, keeping your opinion optimistic and focusing on the opportunities these developments present.

'What are you looking for in a job?'

Consider what you can give as well as what you can get. Most sales people look for challenge and opportunity, so as well as increased commission, consider the challenge of increasing orders and exceeding targets, and the opportunity to make sales and increase profits. For example:

> I'm looking for the opportunity to make sales. My experience at [*your current job*] has shown me I have a talent for [*sales, marketing, telesales, etc*]. I believe that's demonstrated by [*your main achievements*]. I'm looking for the opportunity to continue to achieve at that level and beyond, in a company [*with a first-rate product, or whatever the key attraction is*]. I believe your company offers just such an opportunity.

'What are your greatest achievements?'

'What are your outstanding qualities?'

'What are your greatest strengths?'

'What can you bring to the job?'

Your greatest strength is your ability to sell. Your outstanding qualities are the characteristics that contribute to that ability: things like perseverance, integrity, drive, initiative, product knowledge and so on. Demonstrate these by saying, for example:

> I believe my ability to sell is my greatest strength. I have x years' experience working in [*your field of work*] and my knowledge of [*a key product, market or knowledge area*] means I would be able to make a significant contribution from the beginning. I am [*outline your chief abilities*] and because of that I have [*give your key achievements*]. I believe my current employer would agree that one of my key strengths is my ability to do the job even under difficult conditions. For example, [*describe a time you succeeded under difficulties and the benefit to the company that resulted*].

'Why should I hire you?'

The answer is because you can increase the company's profits. Think of yourself as a product, identify your features and benefits, and sell yourself.

'How long do you think it would take you to make a contribution to this company?'

Most companies expect you to be getting on with the job within a few weeks, and making a substantial contribution within six months. Explain that this was what was expected in your last job, and how you successfully met that target.

'Would you say you had good influencing skills?'

'Would you say you were persuasive?'

Give a SAR-based anecdote demonstrating your skill (see Chapter 16). Choose something that had a win–win result and avoid anything that makes you look manipulative.

'Are you a leader or a follower?'

It's natural to assume the organization wants a strong leader with a confident and dynamic personality. It might also want someone who can listen to clients and be guided by their requirements. Say, for example:

> I would say that I'm by nature a leader, and I think most people who know me would agree. I [*give some examples of your leadership skills*]. However, I've found that to be a good salesperson, it pays to be a follower, too. For example, [*give an example of a time when listening to the customer was beneficial*]. So, on the whole, I would say that it pays to be versatile.

'Are you ambitious?'

Reflect the positive qualities of ambition – hard working, focused, goal-oriented and dedicated – and avoid suggesting you are cut-throat or over-competitive. Say, for example:

> I would certainly say I was ambitious. I have the drive, enthusiasm and [*add your own qualities*] to make a significant contribution to the company I work for. For example, [*give an anecdote that demonstrates ambition: overcoming difficulties to achieve a goal, for example*]. I'm very clear about where I want to be and what I want to do.

'Would you say you were determined?'

'How do you handle rejection?'

Show that you can accept rejection – an everyday occurrence in most sales jobs – without taking it personally. It makes you even more determined. For example:

> Rejection is part of the job; some people simply don't want what I'm selling. I don't take it personally; if anything, it makes me more determined. For example, [*give an example where rejection made you more determined to succeed: how it made you change your approach, look for a new market or new clients*].

'How do you rate your confidence?'

Give convincing reasons for why your confidence is high. Reply, for example:

> I'd say I'm a confident person. I'm certainly confident of my ability to sell, and that confidence is based on my [*pick your most relevant sales ability*], my [*your most relevant professional skill*],

and my [*your most relevant personal qualities*]. Within the past [*couple of years, few months*] I have [*give some examples of your achievements*], so I believe my confidence to be well founded on experience.

'What is your attitude to challenge?'

See the answer in 'Questions for creative jobs' (page 194).

'What is your attitude to risk?'

See the answer in 'Questions for creative jobs' (page 194).

'This job needs someone passionate about business improvement. Is that you?'

It's your job to do more business this year than last; to open new markets and reach more clients; to ensure that customers return year after year and that they recommend the product to others. Show enthusiasm about the improvements you have made to sales figures, customer retention, company reputation and so on in the past. Include actual figures where possible.

'How do you handle stress?'
'How do you deal with pressure?'

Indicate that you are stress-hardy and able to look after yourself. Say, for example:

> I've always been good with stress. I believe it's because I'm good at planning and organizing. I [*describe some of the things you do to organize your work and schedules*]. It means that practical things rarely get on top of me, which leaves me free to put all my energy into [*more important aspects of the job*]. I think I need a degree of tension to focus me anyway. I like to feel that tingle [*or however you would describe it*] when I [*go in to see a client, meet a customer, pick up the phone*]. Life would be flat without that.

'Have you ever failed to reach your target?'

Pick an occasion long ago, before you had the skill and experience you have now. Show how you changed your behaviour as a result. For example:

> I meet all my current targets successfully, but I remember when I first started, I didn't have the experience I have now and I came close to missing my targets once or twice. I had to

[*describe the extra efforts you had to go through to meet them*]. It meant I learnt to [*include something you learnt: how to plan your time, how to focus your efforts, not to procrastinate*].

'When was the last time you felt angry?'

'Do you ever lose your temper?'

If you lose your temper with a client, you will lose the company a lot of money, so you must emphasize that you never do so. Say, for example:

Oh, I get angry about [*something understandable – injustice, for example*], just like everyone else, but I can't say that everyday pressures affect me much. I can't remember the last time I actually lost my temper.

'How many hours a week would you say you work currently?'

Your answer should balance effort aimed at getting sales with avoidance of stress from overwork. For example:

It's variable. I put in the time it takes to meet my targets to my own high standards, but I plan my time effectively and I'm good at scheduling, so I believe I work efficiently. There are always times when something crops up or you spot an opportunity, though, and that's when it's worth putting in the extra hours.

'How do you plan your workload?'

'How do you schedule your sales trips?'

Indicate that you spend as much time as possible on productive work, and minimize non-productive things like keeping records and travelling. Explain how you achieve this and illustrate with examples.

'Describe a difficult problem you have had to deal with.'

'Describe a difficult sale you have made.'

Choose a challenging sale and describe the skill, experience and personal qualities you used to achieve success. Avoid anything that suggests you have problems getting on with people or following management decisions. Be prepared for the interviewer to ask about a time when you were less successful. Pick an example from early in your career, and include the valuable lesson you learnt from the experience.

'What do you think is the key to successful negotiation?'

'What is your approach to selling?'

Have a clear opinion. Good answers include cooperation, motivation, customer-led negotiation and win–win formulas. Give an example of a time you applied your principles successfully.

'What are your views on customer service?'

Customer service is a high priority, so show you are aware of that. For example:

> I would say I put customer service at the top of my priorities. Happy customers buy, unhappy ones don't. For example, [*give a couple of anecdotes about times you have dealt successfully with difficult, demanding or angry customers or clients*].

'What motivates you in your job?'

It is acceptable to give money as one motive; it's why so many sales jobs include commission. Give a broader motivation as well, though. For example:

> I like winning [*for example*]. When I do my job well, listen to clients, meet all their needs and objections and make that sale, I feel an enormous sense of achievement.

'How do you keep up with changes/innovations in your field?'

See the answer to this question in 'Questions for creative jobs' (page 193).

You will also be asked questions about specific areas of your professional knowledge. You should be able to predict what they will be. They will be based on things like:

- your understanding of specific sales and marketing techniques;

- your areas of experience and any specialized knowledge you have;

- your detailed knowledge of products, markets, etc;

- how you handle specific tasks and assignments;

- how you approach specific situations.

You may also be asked to demonstrate your selling skills on the spot: 'Sell me this pen,' for example. Make sure your enthusiasm and energy come across in all your answers.

Questions for technical jobs

The interviewer is assessing whether you have the technical proficiency needed. As with your CV, the key question he or she wants answered is 'Can you do the job?' Refer back to Chapter 8, 'CVs for specific jobs', for more ideas about what this means.

Demonstrate you know what to do and how to do it. When preparing your answers, focus on your key skills. Review examples of situations where you used your skills, and emphasize your competence in applying your knowledge. Be clear about the benefits of your qualifications and training: what it means you can do, how it makes you more competent in the job, and how it benefits your employer. Also focus on your career history: concentrate on your areas of responsibility and the experience you have gained. Experience brings knowledge, competence and proficiency. Keep these points in mind while you think about how you would answer the following questions.

'What do you know about our company?'

Think logically and intelligently about the products and processes you will be involved with, and outline a short, thorough summary, ending with why the company, its products and technical procedures interest you, and why you want to join it.

'What do you think the key trends in the industry are?'

Outline the key developments as you see them, focusing on the interesting opportunities these developments offer.

'How do you keep pace with changes and innovation in your profession?'

See the answer in 'Questions for creative jobs' (page 193).

'Describe how your current job relates to the overall goals of your department or company.'

Technical people can become isolated, and the interviewer wants to know that you see the wider picture. Show that you understand the relationship between:

- your job and the department;
- your department and other departments;
- your department and the company as a whole.

Explain how your job contributes to the company's overall goals.

'Do you like analytical tasks?'

See the answer to this question in 'Questions for clerical jobs' (page 199).

'What are your qualifications for this job?'

Give an outline of your relevant qualifications and show them in use. For example:

> I have [*your key qualifications*]. I also have [*any relevant in-work training*]. This means [*explain why these mean you can do the job, and the benefit to the company*]. In addition to my qualifications, I also have [*give your relevant experience*]. Because of this experience, I understand [*a relevant area, process, technology, etc*] and am familiar with [*another relevant area, process, etc*], which means that [*describe how this makes you suitable for the job*].

'What are your greatest strengths?'

'What are your outstanding qualities?

'What makes you a good [what your job is]?'

'What are your greatest accomplishments/achievements?'

Your greatest strengths are your knowledge, your technical skills and your ability to use those skills to solve problems and complete projects on time and to budget. Say, for example:

> I would say my greatest strengths are my technical skills and my ability to use those skills to solve problems and complete projects on time and to budget. I believe my current employer would say that one of my key strengths is my ability to do the job even when things get tough. For example, [*describe a time you completed a job or tackled a problem under difficult conditions and the resulting benefit to the company*].

'What are the crucial aspects of your job?'

'How do you define doing a good job in your profession?'

Reply, for example:

> The most important part of my job is [*your key tasks and responsibilities*]. The standard performance indicator in [*an engineering project, for example*] is getting the project completed on time, within budget and to the standard outlined in the project documentation. For me, doing a good job means [*give your personal criteria for success*].

'Why should I hire you?'

The answer is, because you know your subject inside out and have an excellent track record of whatever is important in your job: technical solutions, innovation, problem solving or whatever. Give some examples illustrating this.

'What is your attitude to challenge?'

Think in terms of problem solving, and show how you find innovative yet workable solutions. Give examples of how you have used your skill, knowledge and experience to overcome challenging problems in the past.

'What is your attitude to risk?'

Risk taking in a technical job can cost the company money and time, and even be life-threatening. Show how you anticipate risks and take appropriate action to avoid them. Say, for example:

> I would never take a risk that would compromise the safety of the staff or the reputation of the company. For example, [give an anecdote about a time you were faced with a risk and used your problem-solving skills to avoid it].

'What are your views on health and safety in your job?'
'Have you ever had to bend health and safety rules to get a job done?'

See the answer to these questions in 'Questions for practical jobs' (page 191).

'How do you deal with criticism?'

See the answer in 'Questions for creative jobs' (page 195).

'Would you call yourself a problem solver?'
'Would you say you were innovative?'

Give an example showing your problem-solving skills. Describe the problem and how you used your skill, knowledge and experience to achieve an elegant, workable solution. Include the benefit to the company.

'Can you work under pressure?'

'What kinds of pressures arise in your job?'

The real question is, can you retain your competence, expertise and accuracy while under pressure? Say, for example:

> The nature of my job means that I have to work under pressure [*very often, occasionally*]. The sort of things that can arise are [*give examples*]. I don't find working under pressure a problem; I've learnt to [*say what practical things you do to manage it*]. I've found that it can actually be constructive, there's a tremendous sense of satisfaction when you succeed. For example, [*give an example of working successfully under pressure*].

'How do you approach a project?'

The interviewer wants to know if you are methodical and systematic. The answer should take into account:

- your problem-solving approach to the task;
- resource planning: what you need to get the job done – tools, materials, people, equipment, etc;
- time planning: scheduling what must be done if the completion date is to be met;
- budget planning: allocating money, time and resources to each stage of the project;
- contingency planning: what you will do when things go wrong, including time and cost overspends.

'How do you interact with people at different levels?'

See the answer to this question in 'Questions for creative jobs' (page 195).

'What would you do if your opinion differed from that of your boss?'

If your boss is about to make a decision you know won't work, it's your responsibility to suggest an alternative. You might be the only person with the specialist technical knowledge to do so. Can you disagree and get your point across tactfully? Say, for example:

My current manager is very good about discussing problems and issues. She values my experience, so I usually have some input. If my opinion differs from hers, I try to find out why – what angle she's approaching it from that gives her a different point of view. I explain the reasons I think as I do, and in the discussion we usually find a mutually acceptable solution. For example, [*include an example*].

'Describe a difficult problem you have had to deal with.'

'How do you go about making important decisions?'

'Tell me about a difficult decision you had to make.'

Pick a technical problem and describe the skills, knowledge and experience you used to resolve it, how you approached it and the factors affecting your decisions. Avoid problems that involved not getting on with colleagues or management. Say, for example:

When I have an important decision to make [*or problem to solve*], first I gather all the facts I can [*for example*]. Second, I talk to the people involved and get their input. Third, I examine all aspects and try to predict the possible outcomes. Lastly, I try to foresee any contingencies that might affect my decision along with any problems that might arise from it. When I have all that information, in my experience a clear option usually stands out. Taking into consideration factors such as timing, budget and so forth, it's then usually possible to make an appropriate decision. For example, [*briefly outline the process of a decision you made*].

'Are you planning to continue your studies?'

Adding to your qualifications and updating your knowledge is a positive thing, especially in technical jobs. Tell the interviewer about any additional training you have done since leaving college or university, including in-work training and accredited courses, and any future plans you have to upgrade your qualifications and your value to the company.

Expect to be asked specific questions about your job and your professional knowledge. It's not possible to anticipate all the questions that might come up – they are too technically specific – but they will be based on things like:

- your knowledge and understanding of special techniques;

- details of your technical knowledge;

- how you deal with situations that could arise in your work;

- what you would do in specific circumstances;

- your understanding of specific processes;

- your experience of using particular machinery or equipment;

- your knowledge of technical software;

- how you set about commonly occurring tasks.

As your job is likely to include problem solving, you may be given examples of technical problems to unravel. As with all questions, give full, detailed answers based on real-life experience.

Questions for management jobs

The key question the interviewer wants answered is 'Will you get results?' See Chapter 8, 'CVs for specific jobs', for more about what this means in practice. To show you will be an effective manager, review:

- your achievements, developing SAR-based anecdotes showing you as someone who makes a positive difference (see Chapter 16);

- your management skills, finding examples of occasions you have successfully demonstrated managerial abilities and got results;

- your personal qualities, identifying times you have demonstrated:

  - tenacity and perseverance;

  - drive, confidence and motivation;

  - energy, commitment and enthusiasm;

  - reliability, honesty and integrity.

- Keep these in mind when preparing your answers.

'What do you know about our company?'

Prepare a SWOT analysis:

- strengths: its achievements, reputation, what it does well;

- weaknesses: make sure you are aware of them but don't emphasize them;

- opportunities: potential markets, changing environments, technical innovations and so on;

- threats: competitors, diminishing markets and the like.

Conclude with why the company interests you, and how you can contribute to its future growth.

'What do you think the key trends in the industry are?'

See the answer to this question in 'Questions for sales and marketing jobs' (page 201).

'How do you keep pace with changes and innovations in your job?'

See the answer in 'Questions for creative jobs' (page 193).

'How do you manage/have you managed change?'

Change management is a major part of business. You not only have to adjust to change yourself; you have to make change workable and acceptable to your staff. Answer with real-life examples if possible. Outline the situation, say what positive difference the change made, and describe how you:

- analysed the situation and identified the changes to be made;
- decided the actions to be taken;
- persuaded the people involved to accept change;
- supervised implementation of the changes;
- dealt with unforeseen problems and what you learnt from them.

'How would you define your profession?'

Management covers many responsibilities. Read the job description to see what the company needs. Does it want a problem solver or a motivator? Base your answer on its requirements.

'How would you define a conducive working atmosphere?'

A conducive working atmosphere is one in which the team is productive. What encourages optimum productivity in your experience, and how do you support that? Consider things like:

- understandable goals and outcomes;

- a united vision;

- clear roles and responsibilities;

- a degree of independence for team members;

- positive feedback;

- supportive management.

Say, for example:

> I believe the key factors in establishing a productive atmosphere are [*whatever you believe them to be*]. They are important because [*explain why they are necessary in practical terms*]. In my experience, [*give an anecdote illustrating your successful use of these factors to improve your team's performance*].

'Why should I hire you?'
'What are your greatest strengths?'
'What makes you a good manager?'
'Why do you believe you would make a good manager?'
'What can you bring to the job?'

Highlight your ability to get results and pick out the skills and qualities that support it. Answer, for example:

> I would say I can bring to this job [*key requirements mentioned in the job description*]. I believe my previous employers would agree that one of my key strengths is my ability to get results even in difficult circumstances. For example, [*tell the interviewer about the results you have achieved and how you have achieved them*].

'What would you do if we gave you a free hand?'

See the answer to this question in 'Questions for creative jobs' (page 193).

'How do you go about making important decisions?'

'Tell me about a difficult decision you've had to make.'

'Describe a difficult problem you've had to deal with.'

See the answer in 'Questions for technical jobs' (page 211).

'How do you respond to criticism?'

See the answer in 'Questions for creative jobs' (page 195).

'What are you looking for in a job?'

'What motivates you?'

Most people in management are looking for the opportunity to use their skills and experience to make a significant contribution and put their own stamp on an organization. You could reply, for example:

> I'm looking for the opportunity to make a difference. My experience [*in your present job*] has shown me I have a talent for [*management or whatever is relevant to the job you are applying for*]. I believe that's clearly demonstrated by [*your achievements*]. I am looking for the opportunity to continue to achieve at that level and beyond, in a company with a first-rate [*product, service, reputation*], and I believe this company offers just such an opportunity.

'When was the last time you lost your temper?'

You must stay calm under provocation, but it's important to show that you are no mild-mannered pushover. Say, for example:

> I can't remember the last time I lost my temper. Everyday irritations don't affect me that much, they are just a part of life. However, I take a very strong line with my staff over [*something important – honesty, customer courtesy, bullying, etc*]. For example, [*give an example of a time you had to tackle someone about this problem. Show how you dealt with it reasonably and fairly and maintained a good working relationship*].

'What is your attitude to challenge?'

'What is your attitude to risk?'

Managers need to face up to challenges and take calculated risks when the need arises. Make it clear that when you take on a challenge you expect to succeed. Say, for example:

I believe that meeting and overcoming challenges is the way to grow and develop. For example, [*outline a problem that challenged you. Include details of how you analysed the problem, weighed the options, came to a decision about what to do, and the skills you used to carry it out*]. As a result [*give the positive benefits to the company or your team*] and I learnt [*say how you developed positively*].

'Would you say you were confident?'

See the answer to a similar question in 'Questions for sales and marketing jobs' (page 203).

'Would you say you had authority?'

Show you have the respect of your staff while still being pleasant and supportive. Reply, for example:

I don't have problems with that. I foster an attitude of mutual respect within my team and I'm certain they could come to me if they had a problem with anything. I set clear goals and targets and, where it's appropriate, encourage full discussion and keep them informed of the reasons behind my decisions [*or anything else you do*]. I expect them to respect my decisions and act on my instructions, and I'm happy to say no one has let me down yet. For example, [*discuss a time when you tactfully and successfully exerted your authority*].

A follow-up question could be 'Have you ever had any trouble exerting your authority?' Give an example from early in your management career, and say what you learnt from the experience.

'Are you ambitious?'

See the answer to this question in 'Questions for sales and marketing jobs' (page 203).

'Would you describe yourself as a problem solver?'

Answer with examples of your problem-solving skills. Describe the problem, and explain how you used your knowledge and experience to resolve it, and what the resulting benefits to the company were.

'How do you interact with people at different levels?'

See the answer to this question in 'Questions for creative jobs' (page 195).

'What do you regard as the essential skills for motivating people?'

'How do you get the best from people?'

'How important do you think motivation skills are for a manager?'

Show you have the motivational skills to get the best from your team. For example:

> I think good motivational skills are essential for a manager. Getting the members of a team working together towards a common goal with enthusiasm and purpose [*or whatever other criteria you value*] is vital for performance. I make sure my team have clear goals and targets, and understand how those contribute to the overall aims of the company. They know why their role is important and how it fits in with the rest of the organization. All the members are kept informed about developments and, where appropriate, involved in discussions and contribute to the decision-making process [*or whatever else you do that motivates your staff*]. I also make the effort to understand the personal motivations of my staff, be it recognition, challenge, responsibility, or whatever. As a result they are, I believe, well motivated and work well both individually and as a team. For example, [*give an example demonstrating your motivational skills and your team's resulting achievements*].

'What makes a good leader in your view?'

'Do you see yourself as a leader or a follower?'

Give a balanced answer. Say, for example:

> I believe being a good leader is a matter of motivation. Good leaders are people who can keep a team enthusiastic and committed to success despite difficult and challenging conditions. I would say that I am by nature a leader, and I think most people who know me and work with me would agree with that. I [*give some examples of your strong leadership skills in action*]. However, I've found that to be a good manager, it pays to be as versatile as possible. For example, [*give an example of a time when listening to someone, gentle influencing skills and gentle motivation rather than forceful dynamism got results*].

'What are the key factors for a successful team?'

'What skills do you feel are essential to team building?'

Say, for example:

> I believe a successful team is one where the members are committed to each other and to achieving a worthwhile goal [*for example*]. It's up to me as team leader to ensure that everyone pulls together, and that everyone understands what their role is within the team and how

important they are to the overall outcome. I make sure that individual skill and input are valued not just by me, but by everyone concerned. I encourage team members to support each other to complete tasks rather than focus exclusively on their own responsibilities, and reward the group collectively when they achieve team goals [*or whatever else you do to encourage team spirit*]. I also [*anything else you do to support team unity*]. I believe it's because we're a strong, unified team that we've [*give some achievements*].

'How do you prioritize your workload?'

Most systems for prioritization include something like:

- listing tasks;
- identifying them as:
  - urgent and important;
  - urgent but not important;
  - important but not urgent;
  - neither urgent nor important;
- making the first two classes of tasks your highest priority and deciding in which order you will deal with them;
- scheduling, delegating or deleting, as appropriate, the second two classes of task.

You might also be asked how you decide which tasks are important, so you need to know what your key objectives are in order to be able to prioritize.

'How many hours a week do you currently work?'

See the answer to this question in 'Questions for sales and marketing jobs' (page 205).

'How do you handle stress?'
'How do you work under pressure?'

See the answers in 'Questions for sales and marketing jobs' (page 204).

'Would you say you had good influencing skills?'
'What are you like at influencing and persuading?'

See the answer in 'Questions for sales and marketing jobs' (page 202).

'How long do you think it would take you to make a contribution?'

See the answer in 'Questions for sales and marketing jobs' (page 202).

There will also be questions about practical aspects of your job such as your knowledge of specific management techniques, your areas of experience in detail, your approach to specific situations arising in the job, and your understanding of the responsibilities of the job. The sort of questions that might be asked include:

- 'Have you used MBO (management by objectives) techniques before?'
- 'Are you familiar with Total Quality Control? Do you use it currently?'
- 'What software packages do you currently use for project management?'
- 'What are the main factors to consider when planning for growth?'
- 'What type of appraisal systems do you use?'
- 'What methods do you use to predict future workloads?'
- 'What type of training do you think is most effective?'
- 'How do you organize and plan major projects?'
- 'How do you go about recruiting a team?'
- 'How do you make sure meetings run to time?'

Give detailed, knowledgeable answers that demonstrate the full range of your experience and show your enthusiasm for the job.

Questions for customer relations jobs

As with your CV, the key question the interviewer wants answered is 'Are you customer focused?' See Chapter 8, 'CVs for specific jobs', for more about what this means. You need to come across in the interview as:

- helpful, cooperative and obliging;
- friendly, outgoing and approachable;
- knowledgeable;
- confident;
- articulate.

Before the interview, review your experience of dealing with people. Consider how you have handled difficult situations. Think about your successes, and what you learnt from each experience. Also review your personal qualities. What makes you good at dealing with people in a positive way? Gather examples of when and how you have demonstrated these qualities. Keep these in mind as you answer the following questions.

'What do you know about our company?'

You will be customers' first contact, possibly when they are angry or have a problem. Be aware of the company's products or services and how it wants the public to see it. Is its reputation based on quality, innovation or value for money? Is it traditional or leading edge?

'What do you see as the crucial aspects of your job/profession?'

The job description will tell you what the company needs – efficiency, ability to work under pressure, attention to detail, for example – so structure your answer accordingly. You must be customer focused, so your answer should also include things like:

- customer satisfaction;
- making sure the customer has a positive experience of the company;
- establishing rapport;
- listening;
- whatever else you have found to be crucial.

'What are your greatest strengths?'
'What are your outstanding qualities?'
'What makes you a good [what your job is]?'

Your key strengths are your customer relations skills. Say, for example:

> I believe my greatest strength for this job is my experience of dealing with customers. I have [outline your experience] which has developed [your key customer service skills]. It means I can handle a variety of situations, such as [give some anecdotes about some of the things you have dealt with successfully, using skill and diplomacy].

'What are your views on customer service?'

Say, for example:

I believe customer service is of prime importance. In my last job, 60 per cent of sales were made to return customers rather than new clients [*for example*]. If they weren't happy, they would go elsewhere. I believe that how you deal with [*complaints, enquiries, queries, or whatever is most relevant*] is crucial, and makes a big difference to how the customer views the company. For example, [*give an example of how you dealt with a situation so the customer was left with a positive image of the company*].

'Do you enjoy dealing with people?'

Tell the interviewer you even get satisfaction working with people who are difficult, angry or upset. For example:

Yes, I enjoy working with people; it's one of the things that attracted me to [*your field*].
Of course, it's satisfying when people are pleasant and everything goes well, but I also enjoy the challenge of working with [*difficult, angry, confused, etc*] people. For example, [*give some examples of doing this, including the positive outcome you achieved*].

'This position needs someone who is friendly and approachable. Is that how you would describe yourself?'

'What do you think makes a person approachable?'

Reply that you are someone customers feel at ease complaining to or asking for help and advice from. Say, for example:

I believe I'm friendly and approachable, and I'm sure the people I deal with would agree.
I try to put myself in the customer's shoes. I know when I've needed help myself, I've really appreciated [*say what you have found helpful*]. I've tried to introduce that into my own approach with customers. For example, [*give a couple of examples of dealing with a difficult customer illustrating your friendly approachability, how you achieved this, and how you reached a positive outcome*].

'How do you get on with different types of people?'

Say you get along with all types of people in all conditions. Illustrate your answer with brief anecdotes demonstrating the range of your positive experiences with people.

'Would you say you were confident?'

Say, for example:

> Yes, I would say that I'm a confident person naturally but I do a lot to support that: knowing the product thoroughly [*for example*], preparing carefully for meetings [*for example*] and [*other things you do to make sure you are well informed and prepared for your work*]. I've always been outgoing and self-assured, and my confidence in dealing with people has developed with maturity. I have learnt through experience, too. For example, [*give examples of occasions you gained confidence through understanding, leading to a positive outcome*].

'What skills do you think are especially important when handling people tactfully?'

'How do you react when approached by someone who looks angry?'

Include things like:

- being calm and polite;
- taking their problem seriously;
- listening attentively;
- being constructive and helpful;
- using open body language.

Give SAR-based examples of times you used these skills successfully with customers (see Chapter 16).

'How do you behave under pressure?'

'How do you react to stress?'

'How do you handle tension?'

Indicate that you can cope with pressure and have methods for handling stress and tension over the long term. Say, for example:

> I have lots of experience of working under pressure [*tell the interviewer when and where, including the reasons for the pressure: seasonal rush, tight deadline, urgent order, etc*]. I've found it can be really energizing. Having to call on untapped potential is very satisfying when

you succeed. If I find myself getting over-stressed, I [*say what you do to calm down: something quick, simple and effective*]. If I know there's a rush [*for example*] coming up, I [*say what practical steps you take to prepare for it*]. Long term, I combat any effects of stress by [*taking sensible measures such as eating well, taking exercise, etc*].

'When was the last time you got angry?'

In this type of job you cannot lose your temper however much stress you are under. Say, for example:

> I don't find everyday irritations affect me much. I've learnt that dealing with people calmly and politely is more pleasant and less stressful for me as well as for them, and it's second nature now. I can't remember the last time I actually lost my temper.

'What are some of the problems you encounter in your current job?'

'Describe a difficult problem you have had to deal with.'

'Describe a difficult customer you have had to deal with.'

Focus on dealing with people using your interpersonal and communication skills. How did you resolve the issue? What did you learn from the experience?

'What are you like at influencing and persuading?'

See the answer to a similar question in 'Questions for sales and marketing jobs' (page 202).

'Describe how your current job relates to the rest of the company.'

See the answer to a similar question in 'Questions for technical jobs' (page 207).

You will also be asked questions that explore your capabilities in detail. These are too varied and specific to be covered here, but with your knowledge of the job, you should be able to anticipate what the interviewer will ask. They will cover things like:

- your understanding of specific customer relations techniques;
- your areas of experience and any specialized knowledge you have;
- what you would do in specific circumstances likely to arise at work;

- how you deal with actual situations that arise in your work;

- how you handle specific tasks commonly occurring in the job.

Make sure all your answers are customer-focused, and make your enthusiasm and energy clear to the interviewer.

EXPERT QUOTE

We base interview questions on the four or five competencies essential for the job. That doesn't mean we just ask four or five questions, we scratch below the surface as well and go into each one in detail.

ROBERT JOHNSON, AREA DIRECTOR, ACAS SOUTH WEST

EXPERT QUOTE

My dream? I want someone who can walk through that door, sit down and do the job.

MANAGING DIRECTOR, BUSINESS SUPPLY COMPANY

18
Questions for school and college leavers

If you need to illustrate your skills and capabilities with examples from your experience, what do you do if you have just left school or college and don't have much to draw on? Make the most of what you do have, even if it's different from the work you are hoping to do, or experience gained outside the workplace altogether. If you are being interviewed, the company believes you have potential. Prepare for interview by reviewing your:

- **Qualifications**: not only what you have learnt, but how it's changed you: the discipline needed to study, the need to get on with people from different backgrounds, for example. These are useful examples to illustrate your potential skills and qualities. Be aware, too, of how the theory you have learnt fits in with the work you will be doing.

- **Achievements**: duties or responsibilities you have held, any team or individual challenges.

- **Work experience**: weekend and holiday jobs, voluntary work, work placements and work experience schemes. Explore the practical workplace skills that can be transferred to any job situation: punctuality, being responsible, tackling problems and so on.

- **Personal qualities**: Be aware that open-mindedness and enthusiasm can be key points in your favour. Review the highly employable personal characteristics that we looked at in Chapter 2. These are extremely important throughout your successful working life, but especially so now at the beginning of your career.

They are important because they predict your potential and your potential may well be the best thing you have to offer at this stage. Your general attitude, character and motivation are the key to your employability. Remember: 88 per cent of employers considered good personal characteristics to be as important as or more important than academic ones.

'Why did you choose the course/subjects you did?'

'Why did you choose the college/university you did?'

Give reasons that show you can analyse and evaluate information and come to a decision. Present your choice as a considered course of action rather than an impulsive one:

- Describe the process you went through to decide which course or college was right for you.

- Outline the factors you considered, how you researched information, talked to people, weighed the pros and cons and reached a decision.

- Give three or four specific reasons why you chose the course/college you did. Focus on career-related aspects: what it would enable you to do, how it would develop your strengths and talents.

- Describe how the course challenged you, and the skills and qualities you developed as a result.

'What were your favourite subjects?'

'Which aspects of the course interested you most?'

Choose something that has relevance to the job you are applying for. Speak enthusiastically and tell the interviewer if you followed it up in your own time, demonstrating initiative, energy and commitment.

'Do you feel your education prepared you for the workplace?'

'What have you learnt that you think would be useful here?'

Outline the relevant knowledge and skills you learnt, and explain how the course taught you not only specific facts, but also how to learn. Describe how education has matured and developed you – opened your mind, presented you with challenges and given you a sense of responsibility – and how it taught you practical things like self-discipline, organization, prioritizing, and meeting targets and deadlines.

Describe how you developed useful communication and interpersonal skills through getting on with people from different backgrounds, taking part in discussions and giving your point of view, and giving presentations to classes or groups. Include any experience of working in a team or being in a position of leadership. Stress your eagerness to put theory into practice.

'What did you like about your weekend/holiday job?'

If the job included tasks relevant to the job you are applying for, focus on those. Otherwise, mention things like:

- doing a good job;
- being part of a team;
- learning new skills;
- being given responsibility;
- working with the public;
- rising to a challenge, tackling a difficult task.

'What did you like least about your weekend/holiday job?'

Don't say it was boring. You can say that it isn't the type of work you intend to do in the future, but it taught you things you believe will be useful in any job. Say how much you are looking forward to getting started in your real career.

'What are you looking for in a job?'

You are looking for the chance to start in your chosen career. You are eager to take the theoretical knowledge and skills you have acquired and put them into practice, and to learn the new skills necessary to make a valid contribution even at a junior level. Explain why the position you are being interviewed for offers all those things.

'Why do you think you would like this type of work?'

'What makes you think you will be successful in this field?'

Read the job description and match your talents, qualities and training with what's required. For example:

I understand this job needs someone who is [*give two or three of the qualities required*]; who has [*two or three of the skills needed*]; and has [*the training and/or qualifications asked for*]. I believe I fulfil those requirements very well. I have [*outline your personal qualities, skills and talents and illustrate them with examples of times you have demonstrated them*]. I also have [*outline your training*] which has taught me [*mention a key factor*]. I am sure with the support and training of this company, I could eventually make a real contribution.

'How do you feel about starting at the bottom?'

However good your qualifications, you will start near the bottom. Reply that it doesn't trouble you. Say, for example:

I appreciate that everyone has to start at the bottom, if only to get to know the ropes. So no, I don't mind that. I certainly hope to work my way up, though.

'How do you feel about routine work?'

Most jobs involve an element of routine, and entry-level ones have more than most. Show your willingness to tackle it. Say, for example:

I appreciate that quite a lot of the work will be routine. I'm not worried about that, it gives me a chance to find my feet and get to know the job. Hopefully, the routine tasks will become more responsible as I progress and develop and become more useful to the company.

'How do you get on with other people?'

The interviewer is worried you will only mix with other young people. Reassure him or her that you get on well with people of all ages and backgrounds. Say, for example:

I believe I get on well with others, and I think people who know me would agree. I have had to get on with people from different backgrounds in [*give an environment where you've had to do this: college, travelling, voluntary work*]. I feel I'm adaptable and open to new experience, which helps. For example [*give an anecdote about your ability to communicate in difficult or daunting circumstances: overcoming language difficulties abroad, for example*].

'Have you ever worked under pressure? How did you cope with it?'

Consider the pressures you have faced – exams for example – and focus on how you coped, rather than on how stressful it was. The interviewer wants to know:

- what the pressure was: briefly outline the circumstances;

- how you coped with it;

- whether you have ways of handling stress over the long term.

Say, for example:

> I've experienced working under pressure [*taking my A levels, sitting my finals, for example*]. I kept things manageable by [*being organized, planning, prioritizing, etc*]. I find it useful to [*say what practical steps you take: reviewing what needs to be done, breaking it down into manageable steps, and so on*]. I've found, in fact, an element of tension can be energizing. Using untapped capability is very satisfying [*include a brief anecdote about a time you did that. Give a non-exam example if possible: a sport or some other challenge*]. If I find myself getting over-stressed, I [*say what you do to calm down: something simple and effective*], and I [*take sensible measures such as eating well, taking exercise, etc*].

'Where do you see yourself in five years' time?'

If you have researched the career you are entering, you will have an idea of where you should be. Say, for example:

> Ideally, in five years' time I would like to be [*what you reasonably expect to be doing*]. I think I have the [*skills and abilities*] to achieve that, especially with [*requirements such as further training, experience, specific professional qualifications, etc*]. I believe this position will help me achieve that goal because [*give reasons, such as excellent training programme, opportunities for advancement, leader in the field, etc*].

'What do you think influences progress within a company?'

Base your answer on developing your:

- job-related skills so you contribute more to the company;

- workplace skills such as teamwork, communication skills, problem-solving skills and leadership;

- professional attitude: reliability, resourcefulness, integrity, efficiency and so on.

'What are your greatest strengths?'

Even though you have no experience, you can still emphasize your potential. You can bring to the job:

- energy and enthusiasm;
- flexibility and adaptability;
- a proven ability to learn;
- an open mind with no fixed ideas.

You could reply, for example:

> I would say my greatest strengths are [*two or three of your talents or personal qualities appropriate for the job*]. I believe I've demonstrated them in the past [*give a brief example of using your strengths*]. Although experience isn't one of my key strengths, I have [*give any experience you have and any theoretical background*]. As well as that, I believe I can bring to the job [*the points above: enthusiasm, open mind, etc*].

'What have you done that shows initiative?'

Give an example that shows you:

- acting responsibly;
- using problem-solving skills;
- showing self-reliance;
- planning your action intelligently.

Don't forget to say what the resulting benefits were, especially to others as well as yourself.

'What sort of interests do you enjoy?'

Include things like:

- a team activity;
- something needing self-motivation;
- activities with a community focus;

- positions of responsibility: team captain, editor, treasurer, etc;

- something you are genuinely passionate about and put time and effort into.

Beware of anything controversial.

As well as the questions above, be prepared to answer questions about:

- the courses you have done and the knowledge you have gained, both practical and theoretical;

- details about any project work you have done;

- details of any work experience you have had;

- any extra-curricular activities you have been involved with: sports, teams, special interest groups and so on.

As well as reading this chapter, read the section in the last chapter relevant to the sort of work you want to do. In many cases, you should be able to base your answers on your educational experience and outside interests.

EXPERT QUOTE

Draw on your life experiences. If you have done projects at school, you have done planning, organizing and research. Playing in a team needs cooperation, commitment, motivation and determination. Break everything down into skills; even playing computer games uses IT skills, forward planning, strategy and concentration.

MARK COLTON, BUSINESS DEVELOPMENT TEAM, JOBCENTREPLUS

EXPERT QUOTE

When I'm talking to young people, it's their attitude that's important. I'll ask questions like 'Why do you want to be an engineer? Why do you want to work for us?' I'm looking for enthusiasm – some spark that shows they're interested in the job for its own sake.

TINA BUCHANAN, GROUP DIRECTOR, HAMWORTHY ENGINEERING

19
Interviews and more

Previous chapters gave an idea of what happens at interviews, the sort of questions you will be asked, and how to prepare your answers. This chapter looks at some of the different types of interview you can be given, and the other things that can be part of them. Get the basics – answering questions – right before worrying about the tests described in this chapter, but it does help your confidence to know what could happen and to prepare for it.

Different types of interview

There are a number of variations you might come across, instead of or as well as the basic style of interview. These include:

- screening interviews;
- telephone interviews;
- panel interviews;
- serial interviews;
- assessment centres;
- informal interviews;
- second interviews.

Screening interviews

These are designed to screen out unsuitable candidates so the company does not waste time interviewing people who lack basic requirements. They are usually done by phone or on screen, and questions can range from your qualifications to a multiple-choice aptitude test. If you get the answers right, you attend a selection interview. If you get them wrong, you may still be able to apply again later.

The interviewer should explain what's involved before you start, and if you would like time to prepare, you should be given the opportunity to call back when you are ready.

Telephone interviews

These are usually screening interviews. It's rare to offer a job after just a telephone interview; there will usually be a selection interview stage as well. Even so, don't call until you are prepared and know you will be free from interruption. Make sure you have all the information you need:

- your CV;

- your diary;

- the job advertisement, job description and any other information;

- something to make notes on.

While you're on the phone:

- Make sure you won't be disturbed – if it's a really bad time and you can't ensure there won't be interruptions, ask if you can call them back as soon as possible.

- Speak clearly – don't smoke, eat or drink even when the other person is talking. Phones amplify every sound.

- Smile – it makes your voice warmer and more relaxed.

- Avoid one-word answers – however unprepared you are, give more than just yes or no answers to questions.

- Take notes – they will be useful when you get to the formal interview.

- Don't worry – the person calling you won't expect you to be fully prepared or make the sort of presentation you would at a formal interview, but do make sure you sound enthusiastic.

Job advertisements often ask you to ring for further information. Occasionally, companies use these calls as a preliminary screening interview. If you aren't what they are looking for, they will tell you so and won't send an application form.

Panel interviews

Where the hiring decision affects several people in the organization, they can all be included on an interview panel. A typical panel might consist of:

- the human resources manager;
- technical manager;
- department head;
- line manager.

Each member will have questions that address his or her particular concerns. One person usually takes charge of the interview, welcoming you and introducing you to the others.

- Make eye contact and smile as you are introduced to each panel member.
- Follow the guidance of the panel leader. For example, if he or she shakes hands and then asks you to take a seat, assume you don't shake hands with everybody else.
- Look at the person asking the question and direct your answer mainly to him or her. Include the rest of the panel by glancing round and making eye contact.
- Address your own questions to the panel leader, unless it's something more suitable for another one of the panel.
- At the end of the interview look around, smile and make eye contact. Thank the group as a whole for inviting you.
- Outside, make notes of names and job titles while you remember.

Serial interviews

These are similar to a panel interview, except you have a one-to-one interview with each person in turn instead of all at once. Keep in mind what each person's interests are likely to be when you answer his or her questions. For example:

- **human resources manager**: career background, educational background, training and development needs, salary and benefits;

- **technical manager**: technical experience, technical skills and training, specific knowledge, specific job-related problem solving;

- **department head**: cultural fit, ability to meet targets, contribution to profitability and growth, career aspirations;

- **line manager**: working style, manageability, team fit, transferable skills, strengths and weaknesses, understanding of the job and ability to perform it.

Assessment centres

An assessment centre isn't a place; it's a battery of tests overseen by trained assessors. Several candidates are observed working together in a group on a task that requires discussion and teamwork. Assessment programmes can last from half a day to two days, and involve from 5 to 30 people. Some are residential, and nearly all involve some social interaction such as coffee, lunch or an evening meal. The assessment can include:

- interviews;

- tests;

- individual exercises;

- group exercises;

- indoor and outdoor tasks;

- informal and social observation.

Understand the competencies the organization is looking for, and think about how to demonstrate them. Don't forget you are under observation during breaks and meals, and be on your best social behaviour. See a later section in this chapter for more about the sort of tests you can expect.

Informal interviews

An interview is an interview even if it takes place in a bar or over a meal. Prepare just as thoroughly as you would for any other interview. Let the interviewer set the tone and follow his or her example. Use your social skills and be friendly and pleasant, but don't be drawn into discussing anything you wouldn't talk about at a formal interview.

Second interviews

If you get through to a second interview, the company is seriously interested. Show that you are interested in it too.

A second interview can be anything from a formal meeting with a senior executive to an informal lunch with potential colleagues. You should be told what to expect so that you can prepare for it, and also whether there will be tests, exercises or presentations. Expect to be closely questioned about anything the interviewer(s) seemed unhappy about at the first interview.

Interview extras

There may be additional tests to assess your skills, qualities and specific suitability for the post. These can take place before, during or after the main interview, or they can be on a different day entirely. They can include:

- making a presentation;
- showing your portfolio;
- technical and attainment tests;
- physical tests;
- job replica exercises;
- group exercises;
- psychometric tests.

Making a presentation

If you are asked to make a presentation, you will be assessed on your ability to:

- speak confidently in front of a group;
- present key points;
- explain information clearly and understandably;
- be concise and work to time limits;
- think on your feet and respond flexibly to questions.

Typical topics include:

- a five-minute talk presenting your key qualifications for the role;

- a ten-minute profile of the key issues currently facing the industry;

- a five-minute presentation on what you see as the three main priorities for the job.

You will be told the subject beforehand, and how long you will have. Assume you will be asked questions, and prepare accordingly. Check what equipment will be available, and plan and rehearse thoroughly.

Make a summary of your presentation on one sheet of A4 paper. Use it both as a prompt to yourself and as a handout. It's better to make a few points strongly than to cram everything in. Don't run over time. Some companies will cut you off once your time is up, and you might miss your best point.

Showing your portfolio

You could be asked to bring a portfolio of your work, especially for a creative job. Don't wait until the last moment to select your work. Choose things relevant to the job you are applying for, and treat it like a presentation. Rehearse beforehand so you do it confidently. Whether you are presenting graphics, a CD, PowerPoint production or website, polish and edit it for the interview, practise introducing it, and be prepared for questions.

Be wary of just leaving samples of your work for someone to look at. They could get lost or damaged, and this gives you no opportunity to present the material and to answer any questions the recipient might have. Ask if you can bring the material in person. Never leave irreplaceable originals; always take copies.

Technical and attainment tests

These are practical demonstrations of essential job skills: things like driving, typing, translating and interpreting. Practise so you give a confident performance under pressure.

Physical tests

Occasionally, there are special physical requirements for a job. You might be asked to take a sight test, or be tested for manual dexterity or colour blindness, for example. These tests need your consent, but you are unlikely to get the job without them. You may also be required to have a general health check by some organizations.

Job replica exercises

These assess how you will behave in the job. They include things like:

- case studies;
- role play;
- in-tray exercises.

The rules and aims of any exercise should be explained before you begin. If you are not sure about anything, tell whoever is supervising you. Let the supervisor know about any difficulties you are having: not having your reading glasses, for example.

- **Case studies**: you are given a case history about a business matter and asked to write a report or give a presentation about it. Review your analytical and decision-making skills so that you feel confident.

- **Role play**: this is usually based on a workplace situation. Think about the job and try to anticipate the sort of things you will have to deal with. The interviewer wants to see how well you manage the problem and the people involved. Stay calm and professional, and think about the skills the organization is looking for.

- **In-tray exercises**: these are designed to assess your management and organization skills. You are given a typical in-tray including letters, memos and reports, and you can be interrupted by calls and e-mails while you work. Sort through the in-tray and state how you would deal with each item. A useful tip is to sort everything into three piles:
  - urgent;
  - important but not urgent;
  - neither urgent nor important.

Work through each pile in order of priority. Review your time-management and prioritization techniques, and practise on your own in-tray.

Group exercises

These entail interacting with a group to achieve a goal. The goal itself doesn't matter, it's how you work together as a team that is important. You are observed by trained people assessing your:

- natural role within the team;
- communication and interpersonal skills;

- persuasion and negotiation skills;

- judgement and reasoning;

- problem-solving skills;

- contribution to the success of the team.

Participate fully and be a good team member. Don't take over and boss everyone around, but don't be too reserved either. Avoid conflict. Give your opinion but don't let differences degenerate into arguments. Make sure everything in the team goes well:

- Find common ground in disagreements.

- Summarize discussions so that all team members know where they are.

- Encourage other members.

- Remind the group what their goal is and keep them focused on it.

Psychometric tests

You are increasingly likely to encounter psychometric tests at interviews. They are devised by occupational psychologists and designed to give an independent, unbiased view of your talents, characteristics and abilities.

There are three types:

- **aptitude tests** which measure your natural abilities, and test for specific job-related skills such as verbal or numerical ability; spatial, mechanical or clerical aptitude; logical thinking or reasoning skills;

- **personality tests** which assess what sort of person you are and whether you have the personal qualities and characteristics thought right for a particular job;

- **motivational and career interest tests** which focus on what drives you and what occupations would suit you best. These are uncommon in recruitment, aptitude and personality tests being more popular.

The tests can be conducted on paper or on screen, and consist of multiple-choice questions rather than practical demonstration of a skill.

You will usually be told if there are to be psychometric tests as part of a recruit-ment exercise. Find out:

- what the aim of the test is: is it to explore your aptitude, your personal characteristics or a combination of the two?

- how the tests will be taken: on screen, online or using paper and pencil;

- whether you can use a calculator for numerical tests;

- if a specific type or brand of test is being used – a Myers–Briggs personality test, a spatial reasoning test, etc – so you can look it up and get an idea of what it's about;

- whether the organization can provide you with examples so you know what to expect;

- whether you will get feedback about the result;

- whether the tests will be taken before or after the interview.

Psychometric tests are nothing to be scared of, as long as you are prepared for them. For any type of test:

- Stay calm.

- Tell the person supervising the test if you have any condition that makes it difficult for you: partial sightedness, dyslexia, or even not having the right glasses.

- Read all the instructions carefully.

- Do the practice questions first.

- If there's anything you don't understand, or if you have any problems during the test, tell the supervisor immediately.

Aptitude tests

These are designed to measure specific skills such as your ability to understand and work with numbers, use logic to solve problems, or interpret diagrams.

Only tests that are relevant to the job are used. Your score allows the interviewer to see what your aptitude is for that particular skill, and qualifying scores are set at a level that means you can do the job competently.

Aptitude tests are similar to puzzles. You are asked to do things like select the next number in a sequence, fill in a missing word or pick out a missing diagram. The test is often timed but you can usually answer a few specimen questions first to get the hang of it.

Examples of aptitude test questions

Numerical question
Underline the next number in this sequence:
    1   6   11   16   (a) 21   (b) 61   (c) 19

Verbal reasoning question
Which is the odd one out?
   (a) rain   (b) sleet   (c) mud   (d) hail

Abstract reasoning question
|| is to = as | is to (a) – (b) ||| (c) =

Answers: (a), (c), (a)

There are books and internet sites that allow you to try sample tests. Practise before-hand. Familiarity will increase your confidence and help you work more quickly. You will understand what the questions are about, and be aware of some of the twists: asking for the next number but one in a sequence, for example.

If you don't know the answer to a question, make a guess: you have around a one-in-four chance of being right. (Make sure points are not deducted for wrong answers: see below.) When making your guess, eliminate any definitely wrong answers first.

Avoid careless mistakes in numerical questions by roughly estimating the answer: is it tens or hundreds, where's the decimal point, and so on. This can stop you picking 4.54 instead of 45.4, for example.

Keep going. If you can't answer a question, skip it and come back if there is time. The questions in aptitude tests often get harder as you go. When you think you have reached your limit, go back to double-check your answers and fill in any gaps. If you still have time left, continue with the more difficult questions until the finish.

Before you start the test, find out from the person supervising:

- Is the test timed, and if so, how long do you have to complete it?

- Will you lose points for wrong answers? It's unusual, but it can happen and makes a difference to whether you should make guesses.

- Will the questions get more difficult as you go through them?

- Can you have a practice run before the actual test?

- Can you use a calculator, for example?

Personality tests

Increasingly, employers believe that picking someone with the right personality for the job means the person will be better at it, more enthusiastic, more tolerant of problems and setbacks, and happier and more productive. Many use personality profiling to achieve this.

A personality test is designed to predict how you will behave at work. The tests use multiple-choice questions, questions that ask whether you agree or disagree with a statement, and questions that rank statements in order of preference. There are no right or wrong answers, and the test is not usually timed.

Examples of personality test questions

Would you prefer to:
    (a) help out at a local playgroup?
    (b) gather material for an exhibition about Ancient Greece?

I enjoy being in a crowd of people socially. YES NO

People tend to come to me for advice.
(strongly agree) (agree) (not sure) (disagree) (strongly disagree)

You cannot change your personality, but there are things that help you show yourself at your best:

- Before you start, put yourself in a positive, professional frame of mind. Base your answers on what you are like when you are at your best. If a question asks whether you enjoy meeting new people, for example, think about how you usually react, and how you would behave professionally, not the times when you would rather curl up at home.

- Practise doing personality tests and questionnaires to consider how you react in everyday situations. The better you know yourself, the easier it is to answer the questions.

- Some things are obvious. If the job is in customer services, for example, questions about being with people and enjoying social occasions need a positive answer.

- Answer all the questions. The more you leave out, the harder it is to get a true profile. If in doubt, trust your instincts and go with your first answer.

- Be honest about who you are. Don't force yourself to be the right person for the job. You might be mistaken, anyway, and present yourself as a results-oriented go-getter for a management job that needs someone supportive and team-focused.

Online tests

Online tests are becoming popular, and are sometimes used on company websites to screen potential applicants. They are the same as any other sort of aptitude or personality test, except you complete them on screen rather than using paper and pencil. The site should provide instructions and a couple of practice questions. The tests don't assess your keyboard skills, and the actual process should be simple, but be aware of a few things:

- You may need to enter a code number or password before starting.

- Check whether you can change answers once you have entered them.

- Check whether you can go back and answer questions you have missed.

- Find out if you get feedback, and if so, how.

EXPERT QUOTE

We use assessment centres for recruitment – we find they're two to three times more reliable than an interview alone. Before, we'd sometimes find we'd recruited someone who didn't actually like the job. Now, everyone goes through exercises that apply the actual competencies they'll be using in the job. They can see what it's like and we can see how they perform.

ROBERT JOHNSON, AREA DIRECTOR, ACAS SOUTH WEST

EXPERT QUOTE

When you get the letter telling you you've got an interview, phone to clarify exactly what will happen. Who will interview you? Is it a panel interview? Will you have to make a presentation? Knowing what to expect means you can prepare for it.

We use tests to assess specific qualities that are essential for the job. Someone applying for a job on the shop floor will be tested for spatial awareness, for example. Someone on the commercial side will be tested to make sure they have the necessary verbal and numerical skills. Interviews are scored on the basis of the interview itself, test results, and any other exercises such as a presentation or group exercise.

DEBBIE MACEKE, RESOURCE CENTRE MANAGER, ROLLS-ROYCE

20
Offers and rejections

After the interview, make some notes that will help you in the future:

- the names and job titles of the people you saw;

- details of any useful information they gave you about the job and the company;

- the next step: when and how the company will contact you, whether there will be a second interview, and so on.

It's also useful to make notes on:

- how the interview went;

- the sort of questions asked;

- any questions you found difficult to answer;

- anything you would do differently another time.

Write a letter

Send a brief letter or e-mail to thank the interviewer. It creates a good impression, and it gives you the chance to restate your suitability for the job. You can include anything important you missed out at the interview, and it puts your name at the forefront of the interviewer's mind.

Example post-interview letter

First line of your address
Second line of your address
Third line of your address
Postcode

Telephone number
E-mail address

Date

Name of interviewer
Position
Company name
Address line one
Address line two
Address line three

Dear [*Mr/Mrs/Ms Name*]

Thank you for interviewing me for the post of [*what you were interviewed for*] yesterday [*include the date*]. I enjoyed the opportunity to meet you and find out more about [*the company or organization*]. It was very interesting to [*see/hear something that impressed or interested you*] and to [*see/hear/understand/experience something else that stuck in your mind*].

Having heard about the work in more detail, I believe I could make a real contribution to [*the company/department/project*]. My current experience [*what you do or the most relevant facet of it*] has developed my [*skill, area of experience or responsibility*] and my [*another relevant strength*] to the level required by your organization. I should also add that [*mention anything relevant you didn't include in the interview*].

May I confirm that I am very interested in this position. It offers the opportunity I am looking for to [*develop my career, skills, professional growth, experience, etc*]. I would appreciate working in/with [*your team, department, company*] and believe I could contribute substantially to the success of [*the company, department, project, etc*].

I hope you will consider me favourably, and I look forward to hearing from you.

Yours sincerely

Your signed name

Your typed name

If the organization doesn't make you an offer

There could be several reasons that you weren't selected this time:

- The interviewer didn't believe you had the skills or experience needed in the job.

- You didn't convince the interviewer you understood what the job required.

- He or she didn't think you had the personal qualities needed in the job.

The interviewer might be entirely wrong, of course, but, like it or not, that's what he or she believes. Next time, make sure there's no way they can overlook your suitability. Before your next interview, make sure that you:

- know exactly what the job entails (use the job ad, the job description and any other information you can get);

- have the competencies required;

- can give examples of how, when and where you have demonstrated these in practice;

- can present these examples confidently and enthusiastically;

- display in your appearance and behaviour the personal qualities the organization wants.

Overcome your disappointment and reply to the rejection letter. By doing so, you maintain a good impression and remind the organization that you are still interested in the position.

If you liked the job and felt the company was a good place to work, keep in contact. A similar job might come up soon, and the maturity and enthusiasm you've displayed might put you in a strong position.

Example post-rejection letter

First line of your address
Second line of your address
Third line of your address
Postcode

Telephone number
E-mail address

Date

Name of interviewer
Position
Company name
Address line one
Address line two
Address line three

Dear [*Mr/Mrs/Ms Name*]

Thank you for your letter of [*date*]. Although I am naturally disappointed at not being chosen for the position of [*what it was*], I would like to thank you for taking the time to consider my application.

What I saw of the company at the interview interested me greatly, and I would still welcome an opportunity to work for you. Consequently, I am asking you to keep my name and details on file for consideration should another vacancy arise.

Yours sincerely

Your signed name

Your typed name

If you are still interested after six months or so, contact the organization again by letter or e-mail. Even if there isn't a vacancy, your interviewer may know of something in another department or branch, for example, and let you know about it.

Example letter for keeping in contact

First line of your address
Second line of your address
Third line of your address
Postcode

Telephone number
E-mail address

Date

Name of interviewer
Position
Company name
Address line one
Address line two
Address line three

Dear [*Mr/Mrs/Ms Name*]

You may remember interviewing me for the post of [*what you interviewed for*] on [*the date of the interview*].

Unfortunately, I was unsuccessful on that occasion, so I am writing to you again to see if any opportunities have arisen in the meantime. Although I was disappointed at not being chosen for the post, I was very interested in what I saw of the company at the interview and would still like the chance to work for you.

I am [*remind the recipient what you do*] with a sound background in [*remind him or her what your background is*] and many/several/some years' experience of [*your experience that will benefit the company*]. Since our last meeting, I have [*tell him or her about any skills, qualifications or experience you have gained in the meantime*].

I believe I have skills and experience that fit well with your need for first-rate staff [*for example*], and I believe I could make a valuable contribution to [*the company/organization/department/ team etc*].

I look forward to hearing from you.

Yours sincerely

Your signed name

Your typed name

Keep applying

Send out as many CVs as you can and get as much interview experience as possible. The more you do, the more confident you get. Don't wait for the result of one application before applying for another; keep the momentum up. It's much easier to shrug off a rejection if you have another interview arranged and five or six applications in the post.

Between interviews, look over your notes and review your performance to see if there's anything you could do better, or areas you could work on. Practise with friends or colleagues and get their feedback.

If the organization makes you an offer

Congratulations: all your hard work, research and practising has paid off. Now you have to decide whether:

- you want the job;

- you want the job subject to negotiation;

- you want the job if you don't get a better offer;

- you don't want the job.

If you definitely don't want the job, tell the organization at once so it can offer it to someone else. If you are undecided, don't wait until you have made a decision, but get in touch at once. Be enthusiastic and positive, but ask if you can have a couple of days to consider. Weigh up the pros and cons of your current job and decide whether you want to stay, and at what price. Do the same with the job you have been offered. Is it worth accepting as it stands?

Contact anyone who has interviewed you recently but not yet made an offer. Explain the situation and ask if he or she has made a decision yet. The organization should at least be able to tell you if you are in the running. If you have interviews coming up, make an informed guess about the outcome.

Weigh up the significance of the offer to you. An offer after your first interview is very different from one finally achieved after a dozen tries.

Negotiating the offer

If you like the job but are undecided about some of the terms and conditions, it's worth negotiating to see if you can improve them. As long as you remain polite and good-humoured, you won't negotiate yourself out of a job.

Decide what's important: the minimum salary you will accept or hours you can work, for example. Are you prepared to offer concessions in return: accepting extra responsibility, for example? Reread the job description. If you have skills or qualifications that are more than the organization was asking for, but of relevance to the job – computer skills or a foreign language, for example – that could be a bargaining tool.

Find out what perks are available, what the organization offers other employees, and what similar companies offer. You might be able to negotiate childcare contributions, car or travel allowance, expenses, a mobile phone or a laptop. You might be able to negotiate working conditions too: starting and finishing times, for example. Be prepared to compromise. If the organization can't increase the salary, would you accept a higher commission, increased overtime or a regular pay review instead?

Once you have agreed a deal you are both happy with, the company will send you a formal offer along with your starting date. Make sure you know exactly what you are being offered before you formally and bindingly accept the offer in writing. If you haven't done so already, give notice to your current employer when you have everything in black and white. Notify companies that have just interviewed you that you are no longer on the market, and contact people you have interview appointments with to cancel them. Don't just leave them wondering why you didn't turn up.

After all that, the only thing left to say is, congratulations and good luck in your new job. Keep this book for when you want to take the next step up your career ladder.

EXPERT QUOTE

Research the company – its vision, values and objectives. We don't just want people to come and do a job, we want them to join the company, and that means understanding its culture and environment. Recruitment is a major investment; we hope people will stay and grow with the organization.

DEBBIE MACEKE, RESOURCE CENTRE MANAGER, ROLLS-ROYCE

INDEX

Find out more at www.koganpage.com/ultimatecareers
Twitter updates #ultimatecareers
 @koganpage